Create Money Now

Create Money Now

✦

You Will Make Money From Stocks and Bonds

Michael Buttacavoli

iUniverse, Inc.

New York Lincoln Shanghai

Create Money Now
You Will Make Money From Stocks and Bonds

iUniverse, Inc.

For information address:
iUniverse, Inc.
2021 Pine Lake Road, Suite 100
Lincoln, NE 68512
www.iuniverse.com

ISBN: 0-595-27141-3

Printed in the United States of America

Contents

1

COMMENCEMENT

"Happy Birthday, Happy Birthday, Happy Birthday to you."

Atop Kilimanjaro, a crew sat at a rectangle oak table. Socrates (a Barred Owl) occupied the head of the table with Mogford (an ox) opposite. On one side of the table sat Gasport, the beaver, Augar, the Polish chicken, Luton, the King Vulture; across, at the ready, were the Brahman Bull and Black Bear.

The party disbanded leaving their presents, Socrates and Mogford.

Socrates winks at Mogford.

"Young man, you are three times seven, a fine juncture. Do you have questions?"

Mogford's tail shoots up and its bristles flail.

"I just finished my first week at the quarry and made nine shekels."

"What do you desire to do with the shekels?"

"Mr. Slate, my boss, said I might want to invest in the company 401 J Plan. What should I do?"

"Who are you, Mogford?"

"I am Mogford Oxenham, son of Benjamin the plowman."

Socrates is jostling in his chair.

"Do you believe civilization will improve the goods and services it produces?"

Mogford's eyes wrinkle and his tail sways.

"What do you mean, Sahib?"

"Do you know who discovered wine?"

Mogford's pupils enlarge.

"Yes, the Egyptians, 2500 years ago."

"Who is said to have created iron?"

"They were great warriors, the Hittites, circa 1,200 years past, mentor."

"Able student, can you trace medical records?"

Mogford motions with his hoof, pressing an imaginary buzzer on a console.

"The Egyptians recorded on papyrus 877 applications for the treatment of disease."

"Learned pupil, what does history inform you?"

"Civilization improves and creates goods and services as it ages."

"Do you hold reason to believe man's progress will halt?"

"No, Sahib."

"Do you know who invented money?"

Mogford snorts and his hind legs grind into the ground.

"Oh yes, master. It is burnt into the souls of my ancestors. 400 years have expired since the Chinese created coins to facilitate trade. Prior to coins my former family was currency."

"Dear cadet, do you know man's greatest creation?"

"Yes, his ability to think. *Everything flows from consciousness.*"

"How do I form my wealth, master?"

"Know yourself."

"I have no knowledge of investing."

"What does this tell you, my trainee?"

"I should keep it simple to reduce errors."

Socrates forehead creased, brows cropped, squinting.

"What about investment costs?"

"Oh Sahib, since I do not know what I am doing, I should do it at the lowest expense."

"Why?"

"Without ideas of finance, how would I know when I paid for advice that I received good value?"

"What does this tell you?"

"I want to invest because I believe man faces unending economic progress. My money should work simply and at the lowest cost."

"Good. Appear tomorrow at the Agora. I will speak of a topic that will get you on your way."

2

INDEX FUNDS, THE WAY TO GO

4:00 A.M., Socrates eyes burst and he exits his bed. Breakfast was grapes, goat cheese and wheat bread. He inhabited the economically challenged section of Athens. His home, two rooms built of clay around a courtyard. Two hours of trek bring Socrates to the Agora where he finds a solitary Mogford waving his tail.

"Good morning, my good plebe."

"Hello Sahib, I find the Agora an excellent place to meet. I will see the shoe maker, buy pottery, visit the law court to verify my bill of freedom, and research a manuscript on agriculture at the library of Pantanos."

"Heed what I say.

An index fund is a collection of stocks. The most popular index fund is the Standard and Poor's 500 that contains capital of 500 large companies. Since this fund makes changes when Standards and Poor's adds or removes a security, it has a low expense ratio. *Warning. Warning. Warning.* The expense you incur in investments has a shrinkage effect on your returns. If you started with $10,000 and the yearly paybacks after a 1% investment expense was 10%, over 10 years your fund would be $27,070. If you eliminate the 1% investment expense, your proceeds are $29,891. You have enhanced your gain greater than 10%. Whose pocket will this money look best?

I believe, for a new investor, index funds are an exceptional choice because of the variety of funds offered and their low investment cost.

How much bite of each shekel invested in a mutual fund is eaten up by investment cost?

There are three portions of investment cost:

- The expense-ratio that is comprised of the cost of operating a fund except transaction costs.

- Transaction costs are fees paid to buy and sell securities. This amount is subtracted from the net asset value (NAV) daily. The NAV is the sum, at the end of the trading day, of the securities owned by the mutual fund.

- Commissions paid to a broker. There are three primary commissions paid as a percentage of NAV. **A** shares in which you pay a 4 to 5% commission upfront and 0.25% annually thereafter. These shares should be bought if you intend to hold the mutual fund at least six years. Mutual funds hire portfolio managers who make the buy and sell decisions. The funds results are subject to the knack and luck of the portfolio manager. These people exit their firms for different reasons. Since you cannot predict the date he will vacate the firm, it is folly for you to believe he will remain at least six years. **B** shares do not carry an up-front charge, but you pay a deferred sales charge spread over six or seven years after which they are converted to **A** shares. If you sell your shares before they mature, you will pay the commission balance due. These shares pay the broker 4 to 5 ½% commissions. *Warning. Warning. Warning.* Salespeople have told customers there is no commission in **B** shares. **C** shares levy a 1% sales charge, up-front, and carry an annual renewal charge of 1%. These shares, at times, pay a 1% bonus the first year to the broker. Ask the salesperson if a bonus is paid the first year. Mutual funds offer higher compensation to brokers to stimulate sales. Who do you think pays the marketing cost of the fund? *You pay* in the form of smaller gains or larger **C** shares are attractive because you have flexibility without the up-front investment cost of **A** and **B** shares."

Money is power, freedom, a cushion, the root of all evil, the sum of all blessings. (Carl Sandberg)

"It is OK to pay a financial adviser a 1% annual fee, if you receive fair value. Does your adviser contact you at least once a year? Does he compare your results with an appropriate benchmark? How are your funds rated against similar investments?

Never. Never. Never. Pay a sales commission to buy an index fund. A salesperson adds no value in providing you an index fund because you can easily purchase the fund directly. An index fund is unmanaged, minimal service or attention is required.

Go home, and come tomorrow at the same time."

3

HARMONY

The next day joins teacher and pupil.

"No one can foretell the future. Singular investments do well for a time and fall out of good standing. If you cannot predict which type of paper will reward you, common sense tells you not to concentrate your money in one or two areas, and to spread your assets across a number of kinds of investments. History has recorded if we diversify, we may reduce risk and magnify returns over time. As the market has ups and downs, types of textiles have tops and bottoms.

The younger you are the greater the *risk* you can assume because you have many years to retirement. The risk of defeat in the market is reduced by the length of time you are in the market, if you expect expansion for our economy. A person aged 25 could allocate 20% of his dollars to a small growth index fund where a person age 50 might not want to put more than 5 to 10%.

The closer one comes to retiring one should consider reducing risk; that can be done by shifting assets from equity index funds to bond index funds.

What is your emotional response to failure? If the first year you invest $10,000 in stock index funds and lose $1,500, will you be reluctant to invest the next year? If yes, remember you must commit to a minimum of five years. If your spirits sag after a one year reduction of $1,500, you may want to consider replacing part or all of these monies with bond index funds. Historically, bonds yield 6 to 7%, equities 10 to 11%. If you can be secure in the saddle, ride the range. If you want a less eventful passage, subscribe to the bonds. Bonds can have beggarly rewards or losses, but they have less risk than bolts.

If you invest 50% in stock funds and 50% in bond funds, you will probably bring in 8 to 9%.

I want you to go to the Online Café and comeback with a list of index funds for consideration."

Two hours hence, Mogford finds Socrates discussing an addition to the library with a member of the Boule, a representative of the public in political affairs.

"I enjoyed a glass of spring water as I did my research at the Online Café.

If one desires to participate in the market in the broadest sense, buy the Fidelity Spartan Total Market Index (F S T M X)."

"Did you find an approach for an aggressive player?"

"Look into Vanguard Small-Cap Growth (V I S G X), Vanguard Small-Cap Value (V I S V X) and Vanguard Growth (V I G R X)."

"Dear disciple, can you suggest a balanced plan?"

"Yes. Please consider.

Vanguard Standard & Poor's 500 (VFINX)

Vanguard Euro (VEURX)

Vanguard Mid-Cap (VIMSX)

Vanguard Small-Cap Value (VISVT)

Vanguard Interim Bond (VBIIX)"

"Accomplished student, what say you for a conservative soul seeking income?"

"Try the Vanguard Total Bond Index Fund (VBMFX) for tranquility."

"If you follow the index fund track, bolts or bonds, you will probably do better than most, including professionals."

Money is the moment to me. Money is my mood. (Andy Warhol)

4

LIFE INSURANCE

MONEY IS BETTER THAN POVERTY,
IF ONLY FOR FINANCIAL REASONS.

—WOODY ALLEN

We move fifteen years forward and find Mogford married.

"Good to see you Mogford, how have you been?"

"I am well, thank you. I seek your wise counsel on life insurance and annuities. I own a motel that has a large mortgage and Mrs. Oxenham wants protection for herself and the little Oxenhams, if Vishnu calls."

"How long do you need the coverage?"

"There are baby Oxenhams; 20 to 25 years should do it."

"You can buy 20 year term insurance that has no residual value.

Term is similar to renting an apartment. You pay an annual premium and after 20 years the policy is renewable at your attained age."

"I bet the premium will be a lot higher because I am closer to meeting Vishnu?"

"Yes."

"Is there another type of life insurance?"

"Yes, my recruit, there is permanent insurance that continues to age 95."

"Why to 95? I may not make it."

"The cash value in the policy will equal the face amount when you reach 95."

"Do you mean if I buy a $100,000 policy, and make the required payments the cash value of the policy will be $100,000 at 95?"

"Yes."

"Sahib, what are the attributes of cash value permanent insurance?"

"The premiums are three to eight times as large as term insurance and they remain level independent of age. Although the premium is designed to be level it

7

is not guaranteed on policies dependent on investment results. The cash value counters the policy death benefit."

"How?"

"If a $500,000 policy has a cash value of $100,000, the death benefit is $400,000."

"Master, tell me about income taxes."

"When you die, the proceeds are tax free. During the accumulation interval, the earnings on your cash value are tax-deferred."

"If I withdraw my cash value, do I pay income tax on the earnings?"

"Yes."

"I heard that Universal Life does not fix the premium; it is a riskier than Whole Life that guarantees the premium. Is this true?"

"No. Universal Life premiums are lower than Whole Life premiums. If you compare the same base premium for the policy, you will find the Universal Life is not riskier."

"Do interest rates effect permanent policies?"

"Indeed, my freshman, in the 1970's when rates were high people bought Universal Life believing the policies could be paid in ten years based on projections of high interest rates. As rates declined, they were disappointed."

"Oh, sire, one has to be *wary of interest rate projections.*"

"Yes."

"Does Universal Life have an advantage over Whole Life?"

"Yes. The premiums are flexible. If you are unable to pay it does not create a policy loan, as is the case with Whole Life."

"How is Variable Life different?"

"Variable Life invests in mutual funds, which add an additional 1.25% average mutual fund fee."

"What are the other ways my premium is sliced?"

"The carrier charges a mortality fee to cover the expense of you dying. There are administrative expenses for issuance and maintenance of the policy of which sales charges would claim plump share. The majority of your premium goes to building cash value but not until a number of years."

"Why does it take that long for my money to build?"

"A good part of the sales charges come off the top and up-front."

"Why have Variable Life policies become popular?"

"Many people believe stows will outperform bonds. If one buys Universal Life, the cash value is invested in bonds. With Variable Life, you choose from a list of mutual funds."

"Are there share and bond funds to choose from? Are bond funds a good choice?"

"Dear flyweight, if you pick a bond fund you will be better served by considering Universal Life."

"Why?"

"The Universal Life carrier will invest in bonds at less cost to you."

"Do you believe a Variable Life policy fueled through equity will have better returns than Universal Life?"

"Since we are bound by the inability to see the future, we cannot answer the question. You may recall that when we up the expense of an investment, we heighten the risk."

"What would you suggest about how to choose the mutual funds?"

"Review the section on mutual funds."

"I do not know if Variable Life is a good idea. If my mutual funds take a hit, my protection will be reduced."

"True and your premiums will inflate."

"Why?"

"When you start the policy you will receive an illustration that will use projections for 5, 10, 20 year periods. An annual target premium will be stated based on these projections. If your mutual fund incurs a large setback, you'll be asked to pay a higher annual premium."

"Over what period of time does the carrier review the fund performance?"

"Three years, but they can do it annually if a steep fall in value occurs."

"They have to raise my premiums to support the death benefit?"

"Yes. You are putting gamble into your need for life insurance. The prospect of mixing gamble and insurance is disturbing. If you die in a down market, Mrs. Oxenham may receive a reduced benefit."

"I see there is great danger in these policies. One has to monitor the results of the funds, and be prepared to post higher premium in a meager market."

"Yes."

"Can I avoid the volatility and uncertainty of a Variable Life policy?"

"Yes. We have talked about a defined benefit policy where market value declines will bring an upward adjusted premium. You can buy a defined contribution policy where the ups and downs of the market will not affect premium, but will affect the cash value and death benefits. This policy begins with a minimum death benefit that will increase with rising investment returns."

"I see an analogy between Variable Life and Universal Life."

"Oh."

"If one wants to keep things simple, buy Universal Life. If one desires to be actively involved, a defined contribution Variable Life policy is easier and safer to monitor than a defined benefit policy."

"We should address risk tolerance regarding the mutual funds in the policy."

"Sahib, what do you mean?"

"Observe how the risk exposure of a life policy fits with other investments."

"How?"

"Your age, if you are younger you can assume the greater risk of a Variable Life policy. If you are past 50, a Universal Life policy that has more stable earnings because of its bond investments may be best. If you have few dollars in fixed income, you may want to opt for Universal Life."

"What is an annuity?"

"Life insurance companies sell annuities. One can invest in a Fixed Annuity that pays a specific interest rate over the term of the policy, or a Variable Annuity that will have outcomes tied to the mutual fund performance."

"What is the structure of an annuity contract?"

"There is the contract owner who controls the terms of the policy, the annuitant who receives the money during the payout, the beneficiary who receives residual benefits when the annuitant dies."

"Do I have a guarantee when I give the life insurance company money?"

"The cash directed to fixed income annuities goes into the company's general account that could be seized by creditors. You should insist on a minimum **A** rated company. The money put into a variable annuity goes to the mutual fund that cannot be recovered by creditors."

"How do I pay for an annuity?"

"You can make a single payment or periodically."

"Are their penalties for withdrawal?"

"If you withdraw before 59 ½ there's a 10% bite on the accumulated earnings."

"Do I pay taxes on earnings?"

"Yes, ordinary income tax."

"What are the payout options?"

"Fixed monthly payments ranging from 5 to 30 years. Lifetime payments lasting as long as the annuitant lives. Lifetime with period certain, example, monthly benefits for a minimum of 10 years. If the annuitant dies before 10 years, the beneficiary will receive the balance due. If the annuitant survives beyond 10 years, benefits will be paid until the farewell goodbye. Lifetime with joint and last survivor payments continues until the death of the last survivor; a useful option for people in close relationships."

"How is life insurance different than an annuity?"

"Life insurance is to provide money if you die too soon and is intended to replace the lost earning power of the insured. Annuities are structured to supplement your retirement."

"One moment, please. If I have retirement money to put to work, should it go into an IRA or an annuity?"

"I believe all traditional retirement plans should be funded before dollars go into an annuity.

"Why?"

"Lower cost. Greater flexibility."

"Explain, please."

"If you bought the annuity through a salesperson, a good amount of your money will be siphoned from your retirement to the pockets of the salesperson. If you bought a policy without a sales load, the cost to administer the contract plus a reasonable rake-off will be charged to you; these costs will reduce your retirement fund."

"I have been offered an annuity contract that has an option that guarantees a 7% annualized giveback for the first 10 years of the policy. What do you think?"

"Do you have to annuitize the contract after 10 years to capture your guaranteed 7% bestowal?"

"Yes. A guaranteed 7% payout is attractive."

"Do not forget the additional annual cost of options. These costs reduce your returns."

"Hanabus Boocock told me his company would pay me a 5% signing bonus to buy his contract. Does this mitigate his sales commission?"

"No. The policy has a penalty for early surrender."

"Is that similar to playing blackjack in the casino?"

"Yes. Casinos have offered early surrender that permits you to discard your hand at the expense of half your bet. An annuity carrier will permit you to cash in your policy and charge you a penalty that is dependent on the length of time the policy is in effect."

"How does the carrier cover the cost of Hanabus Boocock?"

"The cost is spread over the surrender period."

"I pay for Hanabus slowly. Is he worth it?"

"Does Hanabus deliver sufficient value to compensate for the large cost he represents? Moreover, the compounded lost income?

If Hanabus's commission is $1,000 on a policy, it could have been put to work for you, and *you* would reap the benefits."

"How does an IRA offer greater flexibility than an annuity?"

"An annuity limits you to their selection of mutual funds, between five and 20. An IRA gives you a choice of thousands of funds, stocks, bonds, CDs."

"My friend Folger put an annuity in his IRA. Does this make sense?"

"No. The IRA is tax sheltered. Folger has wasted his money by putting a tax shelter into a tax shelter."

"Let's get back to life insurance. What do I have to know to get the best deal? What do I look for? How do I compare policies?"

"Do you feel confident, with my help, you can make good decisions about life insurance."

"Yes, Sahib."

"The *belief in yourself* means you do not need the services of Hanabus Boocock because it is arduous to justify his value on a cost basis."

"Correct. Are their life insurance companies that sell direct?"

"Yes."

"What does it mean if policies of the same face value have different premiums?"

"One would have to look at the illustrations."

"What are the illustrations?"

"The illustration describes the type of policy, the initial death benefit, the initial premium."

"One minute, please, a Whole Life policy has guaranteed premiums and death benefits. What is this talk about an initial premium?"

"True. That is assuming the carrier is well-managed and the premium charged tracks the total cost of providing the future benefits."

"Please, make it simple."

"If the carrier underestimates the cost of benefits, it will not collect adequate premium, and your claim may go begging. If the carrier overestimates the cost of benefits, your premium will be excessive."

"What do I look for in a company?"

"A sturdy financial firm that is competitive in the marketplace."

"What are the most important items on an illustration that I should attend to?"

"Total expenses: state premium tax, mortality and expense charges, cost of insurance, maintenance charges."

"What about investment projections?"

"If you are looking at a Universal Life product that derives its income from bonds, the projection will be more reliable than a Variable Life product that is subject to equities for givebacks."

"Can you recommend a life insurance company that will sell a policy to me directly?"

"Call Ameritas Direct at 800 552 3553 and USAA at 800 531 8000. Both companies are rated A+(superior) by A.M. and Company. It will be helpful if you develop the habit of double-checking. Information changes, what is true at this moment, may not be true at the next. When you commit your money, verify that you have the most reliable information."

"Do these companies have a sales department that can answer my questions?"

"Yes."

"Do these people receive a commission if I buy a policy?"

"No. These are salary-based salespeople. They are not directly rewarded if you purchase a policy."

"This is a different relationship that I would have with Hanabus Boocock?"

"Yes. There is an inherent conflict of interest between a commission-based salesperson and the consumer."

"Where?"

"Hanabus Boocock's success is measured by his ability to sell product."

"Does this mean Hanabus is not trustworthy?"

"No. One cannot comment on the trustworthiness of a person without knowing him. It means it is in your interest to be critical of information you receive from a person where there is a conflict of interest. Behave like a scientist. *Measure. Measure. Measure.*"

"How do I select an annuity policy?"

"Have you funded your other retirement plans, including those of Mrs. Oxenham, to the maximum?"

"Yes. I have $10,000 saved from rental income and want to put it to work long-term."

"Follow the steps you would take in selecting a life policy. Apply what you have learned about investing in mutual funds and fixed income."

"I say, I should manage it as though it was an IRA and part of my investment universe."

"Yes."

"If I am buying a Variable Annuity, what are the expenses?"

"Ameritas Direct and USAA write annuities, request information. Vanguard offers an annuity that has these expenses: 0.25% for mortality and expense,

0.10% for administration, 0.3% for mutual fund management. The phone number is 800 853 7107."

"I will contact each company, gather the information, and make the best choice."

"Congratulations. See you tomorrow morning."

I have enough money for the rest of my life, if I die by 4:00 this afternoon. (Henny Youngman)

5

IN SEARCH OF VIRTUE

Eighteen years eclipse to bring middle aged Mogford.

Mogford finds Socrates at the Online Café.

"The primary goal of this work is to encourage you to apply pivotal thinking to your investment decisions. This teacher does not disparage an industry or an individual. The task is to assist you in obtaining the greatest value. This demands diligence on your part.

If you want to achieve better results than most people, you will have to approach your money differently. You can do better than your neighbor. The ticket cost is your relentless involvement.

One approach to active investing is engaging Gasport, a financial advisor for a brokerage firm. He will meet with you to discuss your goals and risk. Most firms do not want to talk to you if you have less than 25 to $50,000 in investable assets. These firms know that small accounts are not worthwhile. New financial advisors are often suffering famine and would be pleased to speak with you. Gasport will charge for his services either by commission on transactions, or a percentage of assets under management. If you plan to buy and hold for the long term, an account based on commission may be the least costly to you. Firms will charge you a full commission, but many firms discount up to 70%. *Ask about the discount you are receiving.* If you are an investor who presumes to reshape your portfolio during the course of the year, an asset based fee may be correct for you. This approach may lower your cost and removes the commission transaction expense from the trading decisions. If a utensil should be bought or sold, transaction fees should not be considered. Brokers have big eyes for accounts that generate fees based on asset balances. These fees are *negotiable* subject to your horse-trading abilities and the size of your account. Gasport is worth each penny you pay for his service. He earns his fee by producing good relative accruements.

The game of investing is measured by your credit or debit compared to a benchmark. Indexes are common measuring cups to compare performance. If your holdings represent large growth and value companies, the Standard and Poor's 500 is the best gauge. If your positions differ, look for a suitable tracking index.

One or two years may not be a meaningful period to grade the performance of Gasport, but his performance should be contrasted with the appropriate basis each year.

Measure. Measure. Measure. Gasport merits his fees, if the results surpassed the yardstick. If his work underperforms the index more than two years, why do you need Gasport?"

My broker and I are working on a retirement plan. Unfortunately it's his.

"Master, how do I find a money-man who is worth the fee?"

"Do you have an in depth knowledge of investing? The company Gasport works for is concerned about revenue and income. Financial advisors are hired to bring in business within legal and ethical guidelines. Gasport is a sales person. Most people will ask their friend or neighbor for the name of a financial advisor. Many people feel they have to know or like the gatherer. Humans believe if the financial adviser works for a large firm, or has been in the business many years, he will warrant his keep.

These methods to find a financial advisor are crippled and place you in an impaired position to make an effective selection. People expend enormous sacrifice and effort to make and accumulate money. In possession of the money they impart inadequate time or effort being responsible for its buildup. If you apply the equivalent energy and interest consumed in getting the money, to making it grow, you will be well-rewarded.

To qualify as a referral source a person must have a comprehensive grasp of investing. Your friend or neighbor is not likely to hold this knowledge and experience. You know Lorraine De Leur from a community function; you like her and she is a financial adviser for a major brokerage firm. What you know and feel towards Lorraine is unrelated to her ability to effectively serve you. Your warm feelings towards her will confound your perception. Money and friendship are best not put in the same pot of stew."

"Godfrey Daniel. How do I find a financial advisor?"

"Educate yourself. Be online. Join the American Association of Individual Investors (AAII.com). Visit Internet sites: cbs.marketwatch.com, money.cnn. com, morningstar.com, fool.com, Bloomberg.com. If you do, starlight may bless your returns."

"Help me; I bought this book because I'm lazy."

"OK. The best sources of referrals are CPAs or tax attorneys who have lengthy investment experience. These professionals advise people who are self-made millionaires who know how to create, defend and expand their wealth. Millionaires are good judges of talent in money management.

A second way to invest actively is to subscribe to an independent advisory company. Standard and Poor's has a plant rating system. If the service publishes a track record, compare it to the suitable index. The attractiveness of Standard and Poor's service is they get paid for advice alone. Their advice is unbiased, and they do not gain if you exchange securities. If you use Standard and Poor's, you do not have to become involved. You will be relying on independent analysts to provide buying opportunities. They will apprise you of shrubs to avoid or sell. Analysts are not oracles with broadband connected to the future. One seeks a consistency of quality research to set you on the road of successful discrimination.

Morningstar.com offers a great deal of free information on stocks and mutual funds. If you choose an independent advisory service, you will need to open an online brokerage account. The online broker may provide free research from Standard and Poor's. You can do trades online from 5 to $30. The American Association of Individual Investors puts out comparative information on online brokerage firms. Several hours each week will be required to attend to your holdings.

A $100,000 mutual fund account serviced by Gasport will have a total annual cost of 2,500 to $3,000. You can use Morningstar.com for free and execute the trades online for under $500. Is it worth a few hours a week to build your *net worth* by 2000 to $2,500 each year? You will *prosper* as the savings compound annually.

Clive Horspool is a Certified Financial Planner who will map out a plan for you based on your needs and risk tolerance. You will be charged either an hourly or flat fee. A good deal of the work Clive will do for you can be done for free on the Internet. Online brokerage firms and Internet sites will assist you in drawing a plan for gratis. When you complete this book, see what type of plan *you* can construct, before you visit Clive.

Clay Lacount is a Registered Investment Adviser who will provide you with ideas for an asset-based fee. He may/may not execute trades for you and should be held to the same selection standards as Gasport. If you retain Lacount, you may want to combine his service with an online brokerage account where you execute the trades. A $100,000 crop account with Gasport, charged as a percentage of assets, will cost $2,000 each year. Depending on the account activity, doing the trades online and using the service of Lacount should cost $1,250 per year. Attention. Asset-based fees are *negotiable*.

When you are quoted a fee for service respond, "I would like to work with you, if you accept a fee of (insert the percentage you want to pay), we can close this deal now."

If you can drive expenses down with an adviser who outperforms the benchmark, you have a complimentary relationship."

Wanted: unmarried girls to pick fresh fruit and produce at night.

"Enter the Prize ring of self-directed investing. This is hand-to-hand combat with an opponent that is alive but you fail to see. A market subject to a meteor of crosscurrent impacts without notice; where hunger and anxiety duel, where a moment of brilliance flips into benightedness. An arena where many people may enter since the pit is inhabited by few winners. To thrive as master of your money, you must overcome the biggest obstacle in your life, *you*. You will develop the emotional and intellectual skills needed to make sound investment decisions.

Answer these questions truthfully:

- If I buy a stock where I have applied thorough research with good judgment and the property declines 10% the first week, do I feel an urgency to sell based solely on price movement?

- Do I avoid selling a mint that has a behemoth gain because I do not want to pay tax?

- Will I watch an asset decline steadily over time, and not sell because the damage is too great?

- Will I fail to sell a stake that has a burly gain, and watch it enter the subbasement believing it will rebound?

- Will I buy a vendible because my friend said he has made money, and he believes it will continue to rise?

- When I have a sizable increment on a trade, do I feel unfed and keep it because I have not made enough money?

- When I pick a flower that flourishes, do I believe that I am smarter than my opponents?

- When my investments are impoverished, do I ignore them, and believe they will pass to profitability?

- If my account is loosing ground, am I reluctant to talk about it?

- If my portfolio is contracting, am I afraid to make changes because I fear greater privation?

- Will I buy a stow because the company is well-known?

- When my investments are vigorously advancing, do I feel invincible?

- Is the pain of a $1,000 loss greater than pleasure of an equal gain?

- If you win $1,000, do you feel it is found money, and are willing to buy a high-risk stake that you would not ordinarily buy?

- Do you believe your portfolio is special, and not subject to calamity as is a similar ledger?

- Can you put a loss limit on a bolt and sell it if triggered?

- Will you accept your mistakes as learning episodes without self-criticism?

- Can you buy a stock when everyone else is selling it?

- If you answered yes to more than six questions (except the last three), you are not emotionally prepared to be the sole captain of your portfolio. *Emotional intelligence*, not logic, will have the greatest influence on your results. Large investment errors are spawned in the cauldron of emotion. You have the skills to be emotionally intelligent. Begin by examining yourself in regards to the eighteen questions.

Being a successful investor is as much about learning about *you*, as mastering the tools of economics and finance. Let the journey begin."

For sale: antique desk suitable for lady with thick legs and large drawers.

"Oh, Sahib, I must decide if I am a passive or active investor. If passive, I am blessed with a simple and inexpensive approach. Take 10% of my after tax monthly income and apply it to my chosen index fund(s) each month. Believe in America. Sit back and relax. By taking 10% off the top I will not miss the money which would find its way to be spent. I will not use credit cards to finance my lifestyle. If I cannot settle the full monthly balance, I will reduce spending. Credit cards exact a high interest rate on unpaid balances. You reduce your financial security because you could not wait until cash was saved to buy the television."

6

VALUE CREATION BEHAVIOR

Time moves and we find Socrates and Mogford at the Agora.

Mogford mopes towards the hardware store and his side jostles Socrates as he passes.

"Excuse me Mr. Socrates, forgive me, I did not notice you in my haste. Have I injured you?"

"No."

"My bedroom needs painting and I am looking for a painter."

"Are you competent to do a good job?"

"Yes."

"What is the cost to hire a painter?"

"$300.00."

"My strong student, consider doing the work. If you do the physical effort and time spent will be history while the $300.00 remains.

Money has an inherent *time value*. You can put it in a passbook savings account and earn 1%, a money market fund at 2%, a Treasury bond at 5%, or a high-yield bond at 10%. The money you own, each moment, has time value. *Risk* is the possibility of misfortune. Reward is receiving value. Time and inflation are components of investment risk.

A six month CD would pay 2% while a five year CD would pay 4%. Inflation is expected to reduce the value of your gain over five years, and that is why you receive a higher interest rate. A low-risk investment will reimburse less than a high-risk investment. Investment caliber corporate bonds have earned 6% while equities have delivered 10%.

Observe the core of risk/reward, you assume greater risk with share ownership and are paid with a superior result. Reminder, I am talking about a minimum ten year holding-period.

Value creation behavior is a power source to harness that can be a wonderful servant or a horrible master. This applies if you earn $10/hour or $100/hour. How much money do you earn hourly? Start with your average hourly take home pay and add back contributions you make to retirement plans.

Let's say you arrived at $25 per hour. $25 represents the value of your time/labor and becomes a basis. Your apartment needs painting. The time estimate for the job is 24 hours at a cost of $50/hour. If you pay the contractor it will cost $1,200. You have to work 48 hours to net $1,200. You paint and net an advantage of $600. After you finish the job, if there are negative memories, they will melt away. The $600 remains, and can be put to work to multiply.

Mogford elevates his brows as his pupils fill their sockets.

One should not take on a task solely to reduce expense or accumulate money. Are you skilled to do a satisfactory job? Do you require knowledge or craft before you tackle the work? If you are equipped to accomplish a good job, do it. Value Creation Behavior (VCB) is not intended to be inflexible. You are a whole person with emotional, physical, psychological and spiritual needs. Good decisions rest on considering all aspects of one's life. VCB is supported by the belief, if *you* prepare yourself, you can do a fine job in many areas.

In a medium price restaurant a couple could have an average dinner for about $60 (add the cost of transportation). One could buy a cookbook, and produce a similar meal for 15 to$20. You may enjoy cooking. The person you are cooking for may appreciate your effort. A meal prepared for your mate can be a path to romance.

Life presents many opportunities. Use VCB when and where it fits.

Try shopping at the supermarket, not the convenience store. Make a shopping list and avoid impulse buying. Consider bulk buying. Employ coupons and compare generic products with national brands. Share a meal at a restaurant. Hunt for daily or hourly specials. Adopt unit pricing at the supermarket.

Do simple auto repairs and maintenance. Try parking at a cheaper lot, and walk. Buy the correct gasoline at the lowest cost. Keep your engine tuned and tires properly inflated. Do not acquire moving violations or parking tickets. Keep a steady foot on the gas pedal and consolidate errands.

Compare the cost of renting versus buying your residence. Lower the thermostat to reduce your heating bill. Conserve electricity in the summer by limiting your air conditioning. When mortgage rates decline, consider refinancing. Request an energy audit from your heating company.

If you receive a tax refund, increase your withholding exemptions, or find items that may have caused it, and make adjustments. You want the cash in your pocket.

Do not renew your homeowner's insurance without comparing the coverage and cost with another carrier. Review deductibles for premium reduction. Examine your auto insurance, and compare it with another carrier. Consider placing your insurance directly with the company.

Enroll in your employer's flexible savings plan. This is a tax deduction because you are using pretax dollars to pay eligible expenses. The amount you place in the account should be used entirely. Unused money will be confiscated.

Contemplate making mortgage payments every two weeks. This will prepay a monthly payment each year that will reduce a 30 year mortgage six years. When using an ATM withdraw the smallest amount you can. If the monthly mortgage payment is $369, round it up to $400.

Keep records of cash payments. You will be surprised of the leakage. If you have a low-rate savings account, and you do not plan to draw on it; look into a Fixed Rate Annuity that will pay you a better rate and defer taxes. Your state comptroller may hold your unclaimed money. Check it out on missing money.com.

Mogford's ears sprouted.

Social Security will send you a statement prior to your birthday. Integrate this with your retirement planning. Create the habit of talking openly and freely about financial matters with your spouse. Partake in dividend reinvestment plans where your dividends buy additional fractional shares. Write a prenuptial agreement.

Devote one time shots of income to investments. Start at age 25 to build a retirement fund and put aside 10% of your after tax income. At age 30 try 12%. At age 40 make it 15%.

After you retire a loan, apply the former payments to an investment. Do not use more than two credit cards. Attend Charles Schwab investor workshops, 800 435 8000. Bring lunch to work. Substitute take out food for restaurant dining. Compare restaurants for cost, quality, and service. Shop funeral expenses before you die.

Use holistic, natural approaches to heal illness before using drugs. Use the Internet to shop commodities, including travel. When reviewing a travel package, break down the cost of each item. Compare this with the cost if *you* arranged the package. View movies at home on cable instead of renting or going to the movies.

Brings snacks to the movies or sporting events. Eat before you go to a sporting event. Check out lower airfares at alternate airports. Think about not hiring a lawyer to buy or sell real estate. Most contracts are standard, and the title company does a thorough search. If you pay a person to do your taxes, review last year's forms, and see if you can duplicate the work.

Currencies are traded and converted worldwide. If you buy an item with a charge card in a foreign country, it will be rendered in that country's monetary unit, and converted to your nation's money at the close of that day. The value of a currency changes as is traded as a commodity between dealers and businesses. In theory when the market says 1 Pound Sterling is worth 1.5 U.S. dollars, it means to buy a constant basket of goods you need 50% more dollars than pounds.

Currencies are impacted by the country's rate of interest and inflation, economic expansion, the debt level, effective debt management and political climate. You will find ATMs are the best method to exchange currency. Know what the currency exchange rates are before you arrive. Avoid money changes because they charge high commissions.

In spending money in a foreign country how do you know if you are receiving fair value? Shun shopping and dining at places that are tourist oriented. Tourist establishments have inflated expense and suspect goods. If you shop and eat where locals go, you will obtain better value. If you desire to buy an item that is common to an area, do not buy it from the first merchant. *Compare. Compare Compare.* You'll find the merchants that have first exposure to the customers will have the highest tariffs."

Money is a kind of poetry. (Wallace Stevens)

7

COMMUNITY VENTURE

The ensuing daybreaks and Mogford wends the way to the Agora and meets Socrates in repose besides a lake. Socrates eyes align towards the trembles in the earth.

"Greetings grasshopper, what occupies your cap this minute?"

"Honorable mentor, please tell me what you know of mutual funds."

"Attentively culled mutual funds that are monitored can reward you. If you are paying Gasport to manage your funds, being armed with knowledge will polish your results. How does one choose from a menu of thousands of mutual funds? Begin with diversification; spread your bets across the table.

Go to Morningstar.com and select Funds on the tool bar. Click Fund Selector. Fund Group is Domestic Stock, Category is Large. Manager tenure three years. Cost and purchase is minimum amount. Begin with no-load funds. Expense ratio is 1.5% or less. Ratings and risk, check five-star fund. Category risk is low. A timeless goal of investing is to couple good gains with low risk. Returns. Select S&P 500.

Remember, if we pay a portfolio manager to run our money, he must better the index.

Few do. Compare. Compare. Compare.

A foundation of economics is what is a product/service worth compared to a similar product/service? If the fund manager habitually comes in scant of the S&P 500, who is the greater fool? Choose turnover less than 75%. Turnover is the trading activity of the fund. The higher the turnover the greater commissions paid which bleeds the circulatory system of the investor. Net assets are less than, or equal to any. Median market cap is greater than 250 million. Tap the show results button.

As of this writing, one fund met our criteria, Dodge and Cox Stock. There are several key notes to absorb. You do not find diamonds among the shells at the seashore. One must be picky with sound criteria. The compelling reason Dodge and Cox was the number one Large Value Mutual Fund was the expense ratio was 0.87, lower than their fellow no-load firms.

Beelzebub. Oh that expense cost.

Investing is about applying crack discretion based on reliable information. Do not tie the knot to an investment. Judgment is a moving, living process. *Observe. Analyze.* If analysis yields a platform for change, do it.

We have followed a disciplined process to locate a select Large Value Mutual Fund. Fruitful investing embodies discipline. Partitions of discipline are learning and consistency. Consistency demands a leveled, reasoned approach to your investing, devoid of desperation. Put aside 10% of your monthly take home pay to invest, and do it each month.

After selecting your investment style, stay with it until observation and analysis points change. We have chosen a Large Value Mutual Fund, the first slice of your pie. Examine your risk appetite. These mutual fund categories are sorted by risk, high to low, in descending order.

Biotechnology
Technology
Communications
Large-Growth
Medium-Growth
Small-Growth
Large Blend
Medium Blend
Large Value
Micro-Cap
Medium-Value
Small-Value
Financial
Utilities
Health
Real Estate
Domestic Hybrid
Convertible Bond

Merrill Lynch has adjusted its investment portfolio recommendation to 50% cash and 50% canned goods.

Time, the brother of risk, must be addressed. The more time you have to reach a financial goal, the greater risk you can assume. If the term is short, you may want to reel in the risk. Your "being of risk" is a journey that will have a changing landscape. "Know thyself" and strive for emotional comfort along your investment thoroughfare. Perception of risk is subjective.

A 25 year old holding a bond index fund could believe his money is at peril while his equal, owning a large-growth fund, believes there is scant risk of injury over the long haul. Your "risk being" will be realigned by life changes such as: marriage/family, occupation, income, health, value shift, and aging. Keep your "risk being" in balance as your life unfolds. Adopt your untroubled investment risk profile, and select the types of funds to buy.

If you engage Gasport, I suggest you consider no-load funds first because they have lower expense-ratios than load funds. OK, you found Gasport, the crème de la crème of money-men; does this mean you scoop your money to him?

No. Gasport is honorable and competent. No one has greater interest in your money than *you*. When the time comes to unwind your investments, you will be alone. This is why you double-check Gasport's work. Review the Morningstar ratings of your funds. Become a frequent traveler on the Morningstar website. Should you pay him a fee to handle your funds? Perhaps. Do you have the skills gleaned from this reading to create a balanced, top rated mutual fund collection?

If you enlist Gasport, will you compare his results with the appropriate index fund?

Exchange traded funds (ETF) are hybrid mutual funds with these differences: they are traded daily on an exchange in the same fashion as a common share, they are passively managed with numerous types of funds available, they are more tax efficient than mutual funds. When mutual fund shareholders redeem shares the fund may have to sell securities to pay the redemption. If the shares sold realize a capital gain, the gain will be passed on to the shareholders. In 2000, and 2001, many mutual funds declared capital gains despite suffering NAV depletions. Shareholders were liable for capital gain distributions despite two dispirited years.

Since ETF are traded on an exchange, you will pay a commission for each trade. If you trade often, the transaction costs will be higher than the counterpart index fund. *Compare. Compare. Compare.*

Since ETF are passive you do not need the service of Gasport, and it is suggested you do the trades online. Visit the ETF section of Morningstar.com.

Risk infiltrates every atom of our existence. At your conception you were at risk for the commingling of genes conjoined by your parents. Your choice of education path was laden with gamble. Did you follow the pulse of your heart, and choose work that would nurture your soul, or a career bequeathed by your parents or society? An unfortunate choice could produce financial success in misery.

In risk based decision-making there is a vital opportunity component. If you choose to be a lawyer because of your purse, while your center lies as a forest ranger, you have lost the chance to embrace your bliss. This is opportunity cost.

The knowledge of risk is indispensable to bring in the beast (do you recall the largest roadblock to your success?). A stake in a 90 day T-bill is risk free and requires no consciousness. A fling in a startup biotechnology company demands study and a stomach laced with iron hoops.

Morningstar rates mutual funds by risk/rewards and categories. Domestic Stock is one of the four categories. A rating of 1.0 means a fund is as chancy as its class. A score of 0.75 means a fund is 25% less perilous. A bug with this approach is the Domestic Stock genre includes hybrid funds that are low-risk with specialty technology funds that are high-risk.

Proceeds are calculated on results considering fund expenses and payments on 90 day T-bills. A grade of 0.5 means the fund's take is 50% less than its counterparts for a given time frame. Morningstar subtracts each fund's risk score from its return score and sorts the funds as follows: the top 10% receive five stars, next 22.5% four stars, next 35% three stars and the lost laggards' one or two stars.

Morningstar provides category ratings enabling you to compare specific classes of funds. The Berger Small-Cap Value Fund has a category rating of four with above average appreciation and average risk. This fund sports a five star rating. You may be able to find a similar fund with a category rating of five that would have above average accruals and below average risk. This fund would have had five-star remittances with less risk than the Berger fund."

The scene is a main hall of a fifteenth century English castle. Two men prance in a sword duel. During a break, one swordsman declares "Did you know my mutual fund has beaten the market the last three years?" "Jolly good show" the other swordsman responds. "It may be time to sell."

"To unearth differences in funds, peek beneath the topsoil. Has Cornelius Card, the portfolio manager, clustered bets in one or two sectors that have been blessed during the examination period? Do Card's top three caches comprise more than 25% of the repository? Has Mr. Card kept the population of the fund in the small-cap value neighborhood? If Cornelius picked small companies that grew into big companies, and he did not sell them; that changes the risk profile of his ledger. Mr. Card may have been riding cyclical equities into the winner's circle. What happens when the rotation inverts?

Calibrators exist to quantify risk. Beta measures volatility of an investment to a yardstick. To calculate Beta you need to know the monthly gains and the accompanying standard. The S&P 500 is the popular comparison for equity mutual funds. The Russell 2000 is an index for small-cap crops, and the Wilshire 5000 is a total market index. It is worthwhile to dissect the benchmark to test if it is representative of the fund in question. If the Russell 2000 is overweight in technology equities, and the fund is light in technology holdings, the comparison is cloudy.

If a mutual fund has a Beta of 1.0, the fund is of equal mutability to its measuring standard. If Beta is 1.5 the fund moves 50% more than its judgment point. Beta is calculated over a three year period. The longer the risk measurement sample, one finds regression towards the mean. Over ten-year intervals, large-growth and large-value funds have returned 10 to 11%. Small-cap funds, perhaps 1% more.

Your results can vary a great deal from above, depending on your fund selection and Card's dexterity and fortune. If you pick a fund with a Beta less than 1.0, you will lose less money in a down market, and make less money in an up market. Lessened risk produces reduced reward.

Alpha is the anticipated payback, relative to Beta, compared to the results produced. If the Beta is 1.1 to the S&P 500, and Cornelius Card effects a 20% rise, he has hit his mark with 10% in reserve. The validity of Alpha is underpinned by the accuracy of Beta. One needs to know the average Alpha of a group in order to compare a member of that group.

Standard deviation measures dispersal of performance in a mutual fund. The span of deviations for ultra-short bond funds average 0.67 while precious metal funds average 25.74. These numbers reflect a wide divergence of values for the precious metal funds compared to the ultra-short bond funds. If a mutual fund moves up quickly, it will descend rapidly.

The Sharpe ratio uses standard deviation instead of Beta to quantify risk. The fund's payment in excess of the 90 day T-bill is part of the equation. A large Sharpe ratio equates to improved fund results compared to the amount of risk undertaken. If a fund has a big standard deviation, it must compensate with higher givebacks to warrant a sizable Sharpe ratio. The power of the Sharpe Ratio is its gauges the volatility of the fund not its relative volatility to an index. Since standard deviation measures vendible and bond fund in the same fashion, we can compare disparate investments directly. The weakness of the Sharpe ratio it is meaningless unless it is compared to its fellow flock. This should produce a more reliable figure than comparing it to an associated index.

Dinner Special: turkey $2.36; chicken or beef $2.25; children $2.00

Estimating the investment risk of a fund can be tricky when impacted by macro-economic forces. If a recession visits, high-yield bond funds can incur large capital impairment where a mortgage-backed fund may experience capital appreciation. The imperfection of risk measures is they are historical. A fund could be clothed in a low-risk fabric and contain securities festering with problems.

Sound investing dictates that there are multiple facets of decision-making. Historical review has shown low-risk funds in the past continue to be low risk funds, and high-risk funds follow the same pattern. The correlation between past risk and future risk is far greater than between previous and forthcoming returns.

The risk measures stated in this writing are quoted for a three-year period. Look at the five and ten-year intervals to ascertain a consistency of results. A longer time-frame can provide a more reliable photograph. Morningstar research has uncovered patterns between the standard deviation and their category risk measures. Large-value funds have a standard deviation of 12.92 and a Morningstar risk-grade of 0.83 while large-growth funds report 16.99 and 1.16. These numbers indicate what one would believe intuitively, large-value is less risky than large-growth. A larger spread crops up in comparing small-value with small-growth."

Man joins his wife for breakfast on the terrace of their seventieth floor Park Avenue duplex. "Dear, our, our, fortune has been lost in the market. I canceled your credit cards and returned your leased Jaguar. We must sell this apartment and move into a trailer park." Her face becomes the White Cliffs of Dover. She places her chair alongside the railing. She steps onto the chair, onto the top of railing, and leaps.

The man watches her body splash the pavement and looks to the sky "Thank you Paine Webber."

"Broad statistics favor the value investor who buys premium materiel at attractive prices. Common sense supports this because when one buys quality equity at a discount, one is reducing one's margin for error. By compressing your limit for error you are reducing your investment expense that may result in enhanced returns.

The two most reliable risk calculators are: the Sharpe ratio that quantifies the funds excess returns over the 90 day T-bill opposite its standard deviation and the Morningstar risk score that replaces the standard deviation with the negative volatility of the fund within its group. A crucial element of risk measurement is the fund's management that is not quantifiable because of human behavior. Cornelius Card has left his signature at four ports, and could not tell you if there is a next ship, where it would anchor. The stability of investment behavior by fund management it is required to access risk.

Each time you make an investment you are stating this is the best use of my money at this time. You are losing an opportunity to invest that money elsewhere. You cannot make investments selections without error and will incur opportunity disappearance. You can amend the errors and avoid repetition. There will be times when you avert buying a security, with or without cause, and that security nosedives. Experience will teach you silliness and brilliance. Do not wander from consistent, right-minded thinking.

Fixed income investors square off with the risk of inflation, the mouse that ate the cheese.

As time rolls along, it will be nibbling in your pantry. Observe droppings.

Volatility, risk, and time are the innards of investing. Price movement describes the memories of the mutual fund. Risk is the assumption of future dissipation. Time is the moment you place or remove your bet. If you bought the Janus Mercury Fund in January of 1998, and sold it in January of 2000, you would be Zeus.

If you bought the same fund in January of 2000, and sold it two years later, you would be a morgue attendant. You can solve the enigma of when to buy by doing it monthly, independent of the market, or your gain or forfeit. The challenge of selling is composed of art and fortune.

A clue of when to sell could be rapid appreciation in the short or intermediate term. The Janus Mercury Fund had total returns of 58.4% and 96.2% in 1998, and 1999. These numbers are extraordinary considering large-growth funds return 10 to 11% over time. "You don't need a weather vane to know which way the wind blows."

Enter the serpent of greed that has felled many a foot soldier. His eyes bulged, Horace Musgrave had the good judgment and blessing to buy the Mercury Fund in January of 1998, and as the ball dropped in Times Square, January 1st, 2000, he drooled at the prospect of another heady year. The Mercury fund lost 22.8% and 29.8% in 2000 and 2001. Horace ignored history and devolved from a hero to a dolt. Do not be like Horace. *Observe. Analyze. Respond.*

Mutual funds collect interest, dividends, and capital gains from the sales of securities. These monies are distributed to shareholders in the last quarter of the year and are subject to taxation. If the fund is worth $25/share before a capital gains distribution of $1, the fund will be worth $24 after the distribution. Your fund may have lost a great deal of value during the year and declared a capital gain on which you will pay tax.

Small-cap funds, value, growth, or blend have outperformed the market from January 2000 to April 2002 that has been a bear market for many other fund groups. Part of the reason for these stellar results is that small-cap funds have been undervalued relative to other funds. These funds offered higher accretion at a discount. In the market money flows to what is *perceived* as a markdown. Today are the small-cap funds a buy? Yes. They remain inexpensive to their brethren. This will change. *Observe. Analyze.*

Found: dirty white dog, looks like a rat, been out awhile, better be a reward.

These are mutual funds for your consideration. Do not accept Morningstar or my ideas, as other than a *launching point for your research.* You want to diversify and balance your holdings. Balancing requires you not to over invest in one or two funds. The statistics of these funds will cover the period of April 1997 to April 2002. The Morningstar risk scores encompass April 1999 to April 2002.

Name of Fund and Symbol	Five-year Returns	Risk Score	Expense
Large-Value			
Dodge and Cox Stock DODGX	16.38	0.53	0.54
Large-Growth			
Harbor Capital App. HACAX	11.19	1.31	0.66
Mid-Cap Value			
T. Rowe Price Mid-Cap TRMCX	15.98	0.43	0.99
Mid-Cap Growth			
Calamos Growth CVGRX	28.58	1.04	1.50
Mid-Cap Blend			
Vanguard Capital VHCOX	22.15	0.94	0.62
Small-Cap Growth			
Baron Growth BDRFX	17.51	0.90	1.36
Small-Cap Value			
Fidelity Low-Priced FLPSX	17.67	0.36	1.00
Small-Cap Blend			
Gabelli Small-Cap GABSX	14.48	0.53	0.30
Short-Term Bond Fund			
Metropolitan West MWLDX	7.00	0.15	0.58

Name of Fund and Symbol	Five-year Returns	Risk Score	Expense
Short-Term Government			
Vanguard VSGBX	6.84	0.29	0.28
High Yield			
JANUS High-Yield JAHYX	6.02	1.34	0.99
Emerging Market Bond			
Fidelity New-Market FNMIX	5.81	1.97	0.99
Domestic Hybrid			
Dodge and Cox Balanced DODBX	13.31	0.33	0.53
Europe Stock			
Mutual European A TEMIX	16.65	0.35	1.38
Diversified Emerging Markets			
Oppenheimer Dev Mkt A ODMAX	8.28	0.89	1.69
Foreign Stock TBGVX	12.54	0.31	1.38
Specialty Real SUSIX	12.62	0.49	1.24
Specialty Health			
Vanguard Health VGHCX	23.83	0.38	0.34

When you read this, time will have passed since the above figures were posted.

Fresh ingredients make a better repast. Review these funds with new eyes. Have they maintained their market leadership? If they have fallen, do you know why? Have there been management changes?

One can construct an effective mutual fund selection process by borrowing from science. When a scientist designs his research he creates a control group that is independent and unchanged relative to the study group. In comparing mutual funds we use a benchmark in a similar fashion. A scientist never measures a result once; he measures it a second time to confirm the first result. Since the foundation of a sound investment policy is filled with numbers, it is wise to double-check these integers."

Wanted: chambermaid in rectory, love in, $200.00 a month. References required.

"What is the relative risk of the fund? If the fund has had above average risk has it had above average bounty? Use the Morningstar risk-score category and the standard deviation to measure risk. Caution. Effective use of the standard deviation demands you contrast funds of similar investment philosophy and holdings. Include the temper of your tummy in risk analysis. Do not buy funds that function as yo yos if elevators frighten you. If you become upset, you will make errors. Errors equate to lost money.

How do the funds benefits stack up against similar funds or an index? Use three, five, and ten-year periods. Has Cornelius Card been at the helm the entire journey? If Mapower Kneebone has replaced Mr. Card, one has a more difficult time reviewing performance. Remember, you are putting your escarole in the hands of the manager. Your financial fate is tied to his/her craft and providence. What is the texture of the funds possessions?

Familiarize yourself with the kinds of securities the manager buys. Morningstar provides asset and sector breakdowns. If Cornelius is running a small-cap value fund, and one of the darling's gallops from $10 to $40 in three months, does he remove his chips from the table or declare, "Let it ride." The charter of the prospectus of the mutual fund will describes the types of securities the fund is directed to invest in. Is the manager adhering to the charter? If Card digresses from his mandate, contrasting will be murky.

How much does the fund cost? What is the fund's cost opposite its peers? If two funds have similar achievement and risk profiles with expense ratios of 1.0 and 0.5, choose the fund with the 0.5. Fund distributions can vary greatly from year to year, expenses tend to be closer to fixed. Weeding out funds that have high expense-ratios relieves pressure on performance.

Look at the turnover ratio reported by Morningstar. The higher the ratio, the greater the commissions paid to brokers. Since these costs are subtracted from the value of the account daily, they vanish from your wallet unnoticed. If a fund has a turnover ratio of 100%, transaction costs will add 0.5 to 0.75 to the expense ratio. If Cornelius actively trades your account, when the cards fall sweetly, he will generate a good amount of taxable capital gains. If your tax ranking is steep, it would be wise to confine Mr. Card to a tax advantage account.

Do not act on what you have heard to this point. *Observe* the complete vista. Differentiate the investment vehicles against each other."

For hire: tired of cleaning yourself. Let me do it.

8

FINANCIAL CALCULATORS

The sun rises to 12:00. Socrates slides his tongue over his upper lip. Beads of brine decorate his forehead.

"Dear disciple, will you join me in feta cheese, olives and grain?"

"Yes."

"The wizard of www.presents you gifts of gratis to manufacture a host of computations. Go to money.cnn.com and click calculators. Click an instrument that will assist you in constructing a budget. Your goal is to set aside 10% of your net income for savings or investment.

A budget is to be viewed as a financial planning tool to assist you in gathering wealth. The money you spend today on nonessential goods and services cannot visit you with children. Go to wsj.com and click the Your Money section. Complete the net worth questionnaire. This is the same as a balance sheet for a business that list assets and liabilities.

To amass wealth one has to manage debt effectively. There is good and bad debt. Good debt is the mortgage on your house because as you pay down this liability you will be building equity, and your house may appreciate in value. Mortgage debt is good because it is tax deductible. Bad debt is interest on credit cards. This interest rate is high and not tax-deductible. The items you purchased with your credit card may have been expensive and nonessential. If your non-mortgage debt load is out of whack, you are fleecing your future.

Use your balance sheet as a guidepost to permit you to reduce debt and start investing."

9

PROMISES, PROMESES, PROMESES

Lunch lasted twenty minutes. Mogford sits on a patch of grass, a red and white checkered tablecloth between him and Socrates. Socrates back is to the lake; he faces Mogford. A chunk of cheese dangles from the corner of Mogford's mouth as he raises the green napkin to clear it.

"Excellent Sahib, is there desert?"

Socrates passes him a leather pouch of figs.

"Thank you. Please impart your instructions about bonds."

"A bond is an investment where you loan money to an entity and you receive a payment of interest and return of principal when the bond matures. Risk free bonds are issued by the Treasury and backed by the U.S. Government. Patriot bonds track with the five year T-note. These bonds accrue interest that is paid when you cash in the bond or it matures. This interest is free of state and local taxes plus your interest will grow federal tax-deferred until cashed or redeemed.

Attention. Attention. Attention. Deferral of tax is therapeutic because the accrued interest grows and works for you as opposed to going to the till of the taxman. This means you are earning a higher yield because of the delayed tax benefit. When you pay taxes you will be paying with cheaper dollars because of inflation. If you use the proceeds for higher education, they may be tax-free.

Compare. Compare. Compare. As of this writing the five year fixed CD is paying 4.66 and the Patriot bond is paying 4.4%. The tax deferral feature of the Patriot bond compensates for its lower interest rate making it superior. If you are concerned about inflation you can buy an I bond that is adjusted each six months for inflation. Patriot bonds start at $50 and **I** bonds start at $100. You pay $50 for a Patriot bond that has a face value of $100 and is guaranteed to be worth $100 in 17 years. You pay $100 for an I bond that has a face value of $100. There is no guarantee of the future value of **I** bonds. Deflation is a falling of cost over time. Part of the rate formula for **I** bonds is six month adjustments for inflation. If inflation does not occur, you will receive the fixed rate part of the **I** bond formula.

T-bills are issued by the U.S. Treasury, and mature in one year or less. The minimum purchase entry is $1,000. A T-bill bearing a 2.5% rate cost $975 and is redeemed for $1,000. *Compare.* As of this writing a 182 day T bill paid 1.872. You could receive 3.25 APR at ingdirect.com in a savings account that is insured up to $100,000.

Interest rates and terms will change. Each time you invest review the rates and the terms. If you have more than a $100,000 to invest consult bankrate.com for other firms offering money-market or savings accounts. T-notes are offered for periods of one to ten years, bonds over ten years. Inflation-indexed notes and bonds can be purchased. The principle is adjusted for inflation on maturity. The interest rate is fixed, and an inflation adjustment may be made each six months.

You can buy savings bonds and Treasury Securities directly through Treasury Direct by phone or Internet. Go to www.publicdebt.treas.gov or call 800 772 2678.

These securities are available at banks and brokerage houses."

For sale: four poster bed, 101 years old. Perfect for antique lover.

"An alternative to Treasury Securities is mortgage-backed securities that offer higher yields. The fixed income market is efficiently tendered. When one instrument has a higher yield there is a reason(s). Mortgage-backed securities are composed of pools of funds that are filled with the payments of residential mortgages. The mortgagor pays the servicing agent who distributes the money monthly to the bondholders. The interest rate movement influences the flow of the money from the mortgagor to the bondholder.

When interest rates fall people refinance and pay back their mortgages. If the refinanced mortgage is part of the pool that represents your bond, you will receive part, or all, of your principal plus interest. If interest rates rise people do not refinance, you bond will pay interest until called or maturity. A GNMA (Ginnie Mae) bond (guaranteed by the U.S. Government for payment of interest and principal) that has an average life of ten years currently pays 1.25% more than a ten-year T-note.

Both of the securities offer the same safety of payment, but you receive 25% higher interest with the GNMA bond. Why? The T-note gives you a fixed maturity date; you will be paid until maturation. The GNMA affords a greater interest rate because you assume prepayment risk. People will refinance in a low interest rate environment, and you will receive your money back sooner. If you invest these funds in similar bonds, you will receive a lower interest rate than your first bond.

Government sponsored enterprises, Fannie Mae and FreddieMac issue mortgage-backed securities. The government does not back these securities. FreddieMac and Fannie Mae are investor owned companies that have a line of credit with the Treasury Department. You should demand a higher yield than a GNMA because of the higher credit risk.

Brokers and banks buy mortgage-backed securities from Ginnie Mae, FreddieMac and Fannie Mae. Financial institutions create mortgage-backed securities. If you buy a bond issued by a financial institution you lack the guarantee of a GNMA or the implied guarantee of FreddieMac and Fannie Mae, and should receive a higher yield.

Bonds with a long maturity will have a greater yield because of the extended exposure to interest rate movement and inflation erosion.

Brokers mark up the cost of mortgage-backed securities to cover their administrative and trading expenses. Selling commissions from 1 to 3% are added. The sales cut is buried in the amount you are quoted. The higher the sales slice, the lower the yield you will receive.

Request a quote based on a 1% sales charge or less. Quotes consist of the expense of the bond (100 is at par, less than 100 is at a discount, over 100 is at a premium), the yield-to-maturity, the coupon rate, the maturity date, an estimate of when the bond will be paid in full.

Mortgage-backed securities come in "pass through" form, as the money is collected it is distributed to the bondholders. These bonds incur the greatest prepayment risk because they are immediately affected by refinancing. Collateral Mortgage Obligations (CMO) are composed of the merger of "pass through" certificates to manage the money stream. A CMO is structured to speed up payment to the person who wants his money quicker, and to delay payment to the person who prefers to receive his cash slower. Before buying, discuss the time frame in which you would like to receive your money with the broker.

Reject buying callable bonds at a premium. If they are called at an amount less than you paid, you will have a capital loss. *Attention. Attention. Attention.* One should buy mortgage-backed securities with money that can remain invested. If you need to raise cash they can be sold easily, but you will be selling them to a broker. The broker has a necessity to buy your bonds to permit him to cover his expenses with an additional 1 to 3% selling ballast.

Compare. Compare. Compare. When buying or selling a security, develop the habit of reviewing two bids (selling) or two offers (buying). You will find differences that will be driven to your pocket.

Wanted: 50 girls for stripping machine operator in factory.

Corporate Bonds

Standard and Poor's, an independent credit rating company, publishes their opinion on the credit soundness of corporations. The highest rating is AAA that applies to mortgage-backed securities. The AAA grade implies it is remote you will not be paid your interest and principal. BBB or above is high-quality debt. The higher the credit rank, the lower the interest you will receive. Do not believe an A rated corporate bond guarantees you will be paid. Once you depart from Treasury and GNMA securities you assume a hazard of liquidation.

Corporations issued bonds that pay taxable interest semiannually. Brokers sell most bonds. Bonds are traded on the New York Stock Exchange and American Stock Exchange. They pay interest at fixed rates, floating rates (rates adjusted to T-bills) and zero coupon that pays interest at maturation. Zero coupons embody a double negative, you pay tax on money you do not have, and when you receive your money it is devalued because of inflation. These bonds are popular to fund future expenses (education).

The buyer of corporate bonds is capturing higher yield and risk than mortgage-backed securities. Corporate bonds come in notes one to four years, notes/bonds five to twelve years and bonds over twelve years. A long maturity brings greater yield and volatility. As interest rates traverse peaks and valleys, volatility is a passenger. Bond tags move based on interest rate changes.

If today you buy one bond at par, $1,000, that has a 6% coupon and one year later a similar rated bond carries a coupon of 6.75%, your bond could be worth $900 because $1,000 will buy $67.50 of interest and your 6% coupon gives $60. If you sell your bond it will be discounted because interest rates have grown. It will be sold for an amount that produces $67.50 less the selling cost.

Current yield is the yearly recompense you receive. If you bought a 5% coupon bond at par, your current yield is 5%. If you bought the bond below par, at a discount, your current yield will be greater than 5%. Yield-to-maturity measures your total prize if held to maturity. Yield-to-maturity is a complete statistic because it factors in if you bought above or below par. If you buy below par and hold it to maturity, you will have a capital gain.

Corporate bonds may be callable. When interest rates decline issuers will refinance. Check the callable provisions before buying a bond. A sinking fund bond demands a company set aside a portion of cash each year to retire the bond. If you desire stability of income, do not buy callable bonds unless you receive a higher yield to pay for the call risk.

Compare. Compare. Compare. Think of your money as energy units. If you are considering buying a ten-year A rated callable bond at par with a 7% coupon, can you get a similar bond without the call provision? Many callable bonds are debentures that rely on the financial power of the business to pay interest and principal. Real estate or other hard assets buttress mortgage bonds. Collateral trust bonds are supported by securities of at least equal value to the bond. Subordinated debentures are behind secured debt and debentures in the food chain. Guaranty bonds are sponsored by an entity with a strong credit rating. High-yield bonds have a Standard and Poor's rating of BB or less.

As you descend the ladder of credit ratings, you obtain a greater harvest to offset the additional peril you have planted your dollars in. High-yield bonds can have a spot in your kitty. Look for a mutual fund with good relative performance, low risk, and gentle expenses. Mutual bond funds reduce the default exposure by diversifying with numerous securities. It will be less expensive to hold individual bonds because they are not subject to the expense ratios of funds. A fund could be best for you because of the smaller initial investment, dividend reinvestment, check writing or other features.

Over-The-Counter bonds have a minimum sale of $5,000; listed bonds come in $1,000 lots. If you want to buy a new bond, ask your broker for a *prospectus.*

Municipal Bonds. Munis are issued by state, local and governmental agencies to build roads, schools, hospitals and other public projects. Most bonds are tax-free at the federal level and tax-free at the state and local level if you buy a bond of the state of your residence. Specific bonds are taxable at the federal level but exempt at the state and local level.

Munis are sold as notes that come due in a year or less and bonds that mature in more than one year. General obligation bonds are backed by the full faith and credit of the issuer and supported by its limited or unlimited taxing authority. Revenue bonds are secured by funds received from tolls and charges or rents. Taxable Munis exist because the federal government will not subsidize projects that do not accrue to the public good. These bonds provide a greater yield to offset their taxability. Bonds pay interest semiannually, notes at maturity.

Tax-free Munis pay lower interest rates than other bonds. If you pay 31% or more in federal tax, Munis may be advantageous for you. Select bonds of the same credit rating when doing comparisons. Visit investinginbonds.com for assistance in deciding if Munis are favorable for you. Many Munis carry investment grade ratings and are considered safe investments. Insurance companies can insure payment of principal and interest. Every insured Muni wears a AAA credit badge making it as secure as a mortgage-backed security. Munis fly in flock as other debt instruments, when interest rates escalate the market marker dips. Check if the security is callable, and if you are receiving a call-risk premium. Munis are issued in denominations of $5,000 (mutual funds have a smaller entry level). You can sell your bonds in the secondary market to a broker. When selling get two bids, when buying get two offers. Commission loads range 0.25–2.0%. *Tell your broker you want to pay 0.75% commission or less.*

Bonds merit a slice of your investment pie. You can start with mutual funds and when you accumulate $25,000 consider individual bonds because they have lower cost.

If you are risk averse you can boost the percentage of bonds in your holdings. This will inject safety and less volatility. Remember, if interest rates move severely and quickly, bond values will tumble, but time will heal if you do not become alarmed and sell. Nothing is gratis in the bond market. You can extend your yield by *negotiating* down the commission loads. If you accept no risk as in Treasury Securities, look for meager rations. If you opt for high-yield bonds, your plate will be full but may flip over. Consider walking the center path."

Dog for sale: Eats anything and is fond of children.

Real Estate Investment Trust

"REIT are securities that are backed by explicit real estate holdings of equity or debt. The prime purpose of a REIT is to distribute rental income. The revenue dispensed is variable being influenced by operational and debt expense, and rents collected. Market forces will determine capital gains or losses.

REIT are a suitable vehicle to diversify because their performance is more stable than the equity market. A recession will reduce the dividends paid and compress the paper price. Subject to your risk endurance and cash demands, you may consider allotting 5 to 15% of your currency to REIT.

From 1975 to 2000 REIT have had a total deliverance (dividends and capital appreciation) of 16.2% annually versus 17.5% for the S&P 500 and 9.3% for bonds. Intuitively, it is a good bet that the REIT had a smaller standard deviation than the S&P 500 that translates to less risk.

One does not know what the bounty of REIT will be the next 25 years. The numbers suggest they should receive your prudent review. You can own REIT through individual equities or mutual funds. REIT must distribute 90% of their rake to their shareholders; a minimum of 75% of holdings must be in real estate, loans backed by real estate, shares in other REIT, government securities, or cash; it cannot participate in high-risk or short-term activities.

Governance is accomplished through a board of trustees similar to a board of directors. Daily activities are the province of a trust advisor or professional management. REIT are cash farms that produce dividends with the preponderance of your furtherance created from the dividends. Since the asset base of a REIT is real estate, you may have the benefit of capital appreciation to combat inflation, unlike a bond that is defenseless.

The value of quality real estate improves and enhanced real estate values leads to higher rents. Before one buys a REIT one should consider reviewing the kinds of properties that make up the holdings. Avoid congestion in one class of property that may be negatively affected by the economy. Observe the local markets inspecting supply/demand, vacancy rates, and the condition of local economy. Look for property type and regional diversification. Geographical regions have different prosperity rates. You do not want to own rental property in a town where time is frozen.

There are three forms in which you receive money: dividends, capital gains and repatriation of principal. REIT are available in the following classes.

Cyclical: Mortgages, Franchise Funding, Project Finance, Office/Commercial Space.
Consumer Non-Cyclical: Storage Facilities, Mobile Home Parks, Retail General, Retail Factory Outlet, Restaurants, Nursing Homes.
Health: Nursing Homes, Hospitals, Medical Office Buildings, Miscellaneous Medical Care, Diversified Health Care.
Residential: Apartments, Mobile Home Parks, Mortgages, Storage, Nursing Homes.
Travel/Recreation: Hotel/Motel, Extended Stay Inns, Restaurants, Golf Courses, Racetracks, Other Amusement Parks.
Business Models: Locally Focused, Regionally Concentrated, Diversified by Type, Diversified Geographically.

REIT are tax advantaged because they are untaxed at the corporate level. For the investor who has his eye on income, you can build part of your house with REIT. Refer to the chapter on equity analysis for ideas on how to choose individual REIT. You can find a REIT mutual fund that will cost you about 10% of your helping. This book will give you the tools to place that 10% on your balance sheet as an asset. Where do you want the money to lie?

Preferred Stock

Preferreds will be our last stop on the trail of income implements. They rest between common shares (ownership of a company) and bonds (debt of a company). This utensil has no maturity date and its market value will change but a great deal less than the common stock. Dividends have priority over common deed dividends but bondholders get paid first.

If the credit rating of the preferred and the bond are the same you should receive a greater interest for the preferred. Credit ratings can be faulty. The best protector of your money is *you*. Use a credit rating as a section of a puzzle. Observe all the kinetics bearing on the preferred. It may be inactively traded resulting in a large bid/ask spread that means that you will not receive a competitive outcome.

One should buy preferred fruit for the yield and not sell unless powerful fundamental elements arise. The investment community treats preferreds closer to bonds than common plants. When interest rates rise the market value of the equity may fall. If the company or industry experiences hardship, the value of the produce may decline. Preferred plants can be convertible into common shares. They will receive a lower dividend than the nonconvertible.

Fixed income investing is efficient; a benefit you receive is counterbalanced by a surrender of a different benefit. The convertible textile gives you the opportunity to convert to common stock, and you pay for this right in the form of a lower dividend. Convertible shares make sense for one who wants to straddle the need for income and capital gain. When paper is issued the conversion threshold is set above the current common share value. If the common share ticker rises to the conversion price, you can convert the preferred shares into common shares. If dividends are not paid the issuer is not in default. Dividends are cumulative and must be paid before common shareholders payouts.

Preferred shares do not have voting rights, but if dividends are not being paid, limited voting power may be activated. Check if the implement is callable or to be retired by a sinking fund. If the shares are callable, you should receive a call premium over a similar quality noncallable preferreds. Dividends can be adjustable, tied to the ten-year T-note and adjusted quarterly.

Preferred paper follows the same Standard and Poor's ratings system as bonds. It is suggested you buy **A** rated shares affording you reasonable expectations of being paid. If you dip below an **A** rating, make sure you receive a high dividend to be paid for the additional risk of delay or nonpayment. Corporations that own preferreds deduct 70% of the dividends they receive for tax purposes.

This market force reduces the yield the individual investor receives because preferred issuers do not have to compete for their dollars. In 1993 Goldman Sachs and Company created monthly income preferred stock (MIPS) that enabled the dividend to be treated as interest and tax deductible. In 1995 Merrill Lynch and Company launched trust originated preferred securities (TOPS) to duplicate the tax deductible features of the MIPS. Interest earned on TOPS is reported on 1099 while interest earned on MIPS is reported on K-1. Since companies deduct the interest expense on MIPS they are offered at higher yields than traditional preferreds.

MIPS and TOPS mature in 30 to 49 years making its life span equivalent to long bonds. They can be bought near $25 per share, unlike the minimum $5,000 purchase for corporate bonds. The yield spread between traditional preferred shares and MIPS it is 50 basis points. Dividends can be delayed five years and you will be taxed as though you received this income. New issues are noncallable for five years. Tax risk exists because the government may withdraw the tax deductibility of interest. Many issuers provide for redemption if the tax deductibility is lost. Adjustable rates MIPS exist along with convertible MIPS. Goldman Sachs underwrote quarterly income preferred shares (QUIPS) that copy the structure of TOPS and permit filing with the 1099. Before buying MIPS, TOPS or QUIPS read the *prospectus*.

Review the yield spreads between the bonds, standard preferred exchequer and hybrids. Check if Standard and Poor's has placed the issuer on credit watch that may result in a downgrading of its credit rating. *Do not buy* this security and consider selling it. You buy a preferred stock to receive income. If this income stream is in peril, do you want to own the asset?

Extreme conditions present opportunities for one who *observes*. When high interest rates prevail, preferred share stickers will tumble and yields will rise. Look for a high quality issuer and you may be able to reap a 9 to 10% harvest.

If you are ill at ease with Cornelius Card, you can diversify within fixed income. The recipe could include: Treasury Securities, mortgage-backed securities, corporate bonds, preferreds and REIT.

Investing is life. What ever you do, it will not be quite right. If you elect fixed income investing solely, the baleful shadow of inflation will stalk you. If you fill up a wheelbarrow of money, inflation will be a lap dog. Get your wheelbarrow and start filling."

German Shepherd: 85lb. Neutered. Speaks German. Free.

10

RETIREMENT TREASURY

The sun trips to 4:00. Mogford's rear legs teeter. His eyelids droop to cover 75 percent of the cornea. His jaw slopes downward.

"Am I keeping you conscious?"

Mogford stiffens his legs and raises shoulders. His eyelids rise.

"Let's walk as I continue your tutelage. Your tuition is dinner and lodging at the Online Café.

A cornerstone of seizing command of your money is to defer paying bills without penalty. Pay your credit card balances in full, online, one day before the date due. A function of tax law is to serve social policy.

Enter the individual retirement account (IRA). For a single person covered under an employer plan eligibility phases out with modified adjusted gross income (MAGI) between 34,000 to $44,000 and 54,000 to $64,000 for married couples. The tax deductible IRA is available to you and your spouse if neither is covered by an employer sponsored plan. If one spouse is active in a plan eligibility phases out between MAGI of 150,000 to $160,000 for an uncovered spouse and between 54,000 to $64,000 for the covered spouse.

A tax deductible IRA permits you to deduct your contributions from your gross income and your investments grow tax deferred. You will be taxed as ordinary income on qualified distributions. A Roth IRA becomes unavailable for individuals with MAGI between 95,000 to $110,000 and 150,000 to $160,000 for married folks.

You invest post-tax dollars in a Roth and collect tax-free qualified distributions. Anyone who has earned income can have a nondeductible IRA. A nondeductible IRA makes sense if you do not qualify for a deductible IRA or a Roth IRA. Your money will grow tax deferred. IRA contribution limits are $3,000 for 2003 and $4,000 for 2004. If you are over age 50, you can add $500 to these figures.

A traditional IRA requires you to take withdrawals at age70 ½ while a Roth imposes no time requirement. You can make investments in a Roth despite being a member of a qualified employer plan and after you are age 70 ½. Deposits in all IRA's can be made up till April 15th for the previous year. If you withdraw money from a deductible IRA before age 59 ½ you will pay a 10% fine of the amount extracted plus capital gains tax. Premature withdrawals defeat the goal of an IRA and you will be whacked.

One may raid the piggybank without penalty for $10,000 for a first time home purchase, higher education expense or disability. Capital gains taxes will apply. Nondeductible IRA's follow the same rules except you will not be double taxed on your contributions. To avoid penalty, within one year after reaching 70 ½, you must begin cashing out your traditional IRA.

The whole kitty can be had or: partial payments estimated on your lifetime assumption, the existence of you and your beneficiary, not greater than the joint life assumption of the last survivor of you and your beneficiary. Firms may have different distribution options. Review these options before you relinquish your money.

A qualified Roth distribution permits you to withdraw money without tax or penalty. If you are age 59 ½ and have maintained the account for five years you can get your money in any sum without tax or fine.

Other qualified removals are: you cease to exist, disability, home purchase ($10,000 lifetime limit) applies to an individual who has not bought a house within two years. The money must be applied within 120 days of receipt. If you tap the Roth cash register before age 59 ½ or the five year holding period, you will be taxed on earnings and be slammed with an early withdrawal bite. If the five year waiting period has not occurred and money is removed before 59 ½ because of expiration or disability, higher education expense, certain medical expenses, medical insurance premiums paid while unemployed or home-buying, proceeds will be taxed without a withdrawal penalty.

A Roth demands good record keeping averting duplicate tax. The account is funded by: annual contributions, qualified rollovers (money converted from a traditional IRA or spun off from another retirement plan). You need to partition funds added via a nondeductible IRA. Unlike the traditional IRA, the Roth does not demand you gather the escarole at 70 ½.

If you deem to observe many years after 70, you can use Roth dollars the last quarter mile. If you bequeath one other than your spouse, you can eschew a large sum of income tax that will fatten your estate. Your IRA can be filled with any negotiable security. Hard assets such as homes, fine art, land, and antiques are forbidden. Before opening an IRA, check with the custodian (broker/dealer) the types of securities they accept.

Monty Widworthy, a CPA, believes everyone should have an IRA. If you do not qualify for a deductible IRA, *do* the nondeductible IRA. Choosing between a traditional/Roth IRA is hazy and demanding. What will be your tax rate at the time of dissemination? The closer you are to retirement, the easier the estimate. Do you need the flexible contribution/distribution aspects of a Roth? You can inject deposits indefinitely and are never compelled to make withdrawals.

How do your non-IRA assets compare to your IRA funds? If the non-IRA assets are large you may not need the tax free distributions of the Roth. If the IRA is the bulk of your retirement pool, you may require tax free allotments. The younger you are the more appealing a Roth becomes because you will have many years of compounded cultivation.

Monty states there is one situation where you should not have an IRA. If your employer provides matching funds to a 401 K, all of your available retirement dollars should go there and excess funds should go to an IRA. When you are offered free money, grab it. Most 401 Ks have a five year vesting period unless you foresee to depart before five years; do not pass up free employer contributions.

Monty says he does not recommend converting a traditional IRA to a Roth unless you can pay the income tax on the distribution (this is considered income and added to your adjusted gross income) from a source other than the IRA. If you pay the additional income tax generated by the distribution by drawing it down from your IRA, you have reduced your IRA assets and will get smacked with a 10% withdrawal laceration. Research done by Monty indicates that if your tax bracket remains the same from inception to distribution, the payout on both IRAs is the same.

Conversion to a Roth removes the uncertainty of the tax rate since your payments will be tax free. Allotments from a deductible IRA go directly to adjusted gross income and may mark-up Social Security tax. Tax qualified Roth disbursements are not income and will not have this effect. The Roth puts more after tax dollars to work that expands the compounding effect. If you put $2,000 in a Roth, $2,000 goes to work. If you put $2,000 in a deductible IRA and your tax rate is 28%, you are putting $1,440 to work.

If one contemplates to be in a lower tax bracket or withdraw the funds within 10 years, a traditional IRA may be better. The Roth is an effective estate planning tool. If the wife is the beneficiary of the husband's Roth, at the time of his expunging his wife becomes the owner of the Roth. She can designate her son as beneficiary. From the father's death to the son's demise, many years of tax free distributions have been created.

If one holds a traditional IRA and believes the securities are undervalued and would like to convert to a Roth, do it. You will not have to pay the tax until the next year plus you have a choice to convert back to a traditional IRA (recharacterize) and avoid the tax. If the account has appreciated, you may be able to use funds from a taxable account to pay the taxes. This is an advantageous situation for you. The value of the account on the date it is converted from traditional to Roth will be the amount to be added to your adjusted gross income for that tax year. If the fund does not appreciate you have the option to recharacterize without cost or tax. If the portfolio has done well, you will be paying tax on a reduced amount and picked up the benefits of a Roth."

For sale: 2 wire mesh butchering gloves, one five finger, one three finger, pair $15.00

"A 401 K is an employer sponsored retirement fund. The employee is able to invest pretax dollars in a mutual fund. The fund grows tax sheltered. Remember, when you can defer taxes, do it. Your employer may donate to the 401 K.

If you were able to put $1,000/year in a 401 K in 1970 in a diversified account and funded it ten years, it would be worth $364,000 (April 2002). If, you began in 1980 and put $1,000 away for 20 years in a similar portfolio, it would be worth $127,000.

Start the power of compounding. *Do it now.* If your employer does not contribute to the 401 K you should first fund an IRA and then the 401K. You control the IRA and you are not subject to the employer plan limitations. Do not borrow from your 401 K. If you lose your job you will have to repay the loan at once. If you fail at repayment you will be hit with taxes plus a 10% removal penalty. When you leave your job you can roll over your 401 K to an IRA. Be certain that the check is made to the custodian or your employer is compelled to deduct 20% for taxes. You must complete the roll within 60 days. If 20% was deducted it will be returned after tax filing but you must add the 20% to the IRA or you'll incur taxes and a 10% departing fine.

A Simplified Employee Pension Plan (SEP) is easy and inexpensive to install. The employer, with tax deductible dollars, solely funds the program. The funding is flexible allowing the employer to vary contributions year to year. An eligible employee is one who has worked three of the last five years and earned at least $450 the last year (all such employees must be covered). Up to 25% of the employee's salary (limit $40,000) can be funded each year and up to 20% of the employer salary (limit $40,000). Vesting is immediate and the employee chooses the investment vehicle that can be any marketable security.

A Savings Incentive Match Plan (Simple IRA) permits employee contributions up to $7,000 with employer matching amounts of 1 to 3% of salary. The employer can fund $7,000 plus the matching amount. Employees who have worked in any two years prior (making at least $5,000 each year) and are anticipated to earn $5,000 in the current year are eligible. Vesting is at inception and employer pairing funds are mandatory. The investor selects which types of securities to buy.

A Profit Sharing Plan is funded by the surplus of the company that can vary from year to year. Employees who have worked 1,000 hours the past year (two years if no vesting period) can participate. The contribution limits are the same as the SEP. Members may not add money to the fund. The employer determines vesting.

A Money Purchase Plan allows 25% of salary contribution. Employer contributions are mandated annually per the elected percentage. Vesting can be graded if the employer chooses a minimum of one year service for eligibility. If more than one year of service is chosen, the employee is immediately vested upon eligibility.

A company could combine a Profit Sharing Plan with a Money Purchase Plan where a fixed minimum contribution would apply to the Money Purchase Plan and the Profit Sharing Plan could be activated when appropriate.

An Educational IRA (EIRA) can be set up to pay for qualified primary, secondary or higher education expenses. An EIRA is independent of other IRAs because anyone can make a contribution if the recipient is under age 18. The amount one can donate is limited by one's adjusted gross income (AGI). Uncle Neville Gubb who has no earned income would like to help his nephew Fuller. This is OK because earned income is not a requirement. Fuller's account can be funded up to $2,000 each year. The money will grow tax deferred and qualified distributions will be tax free. If uncle Neville's AGI prevents contribution, Neville can gift Fuller $2,000 to establish the fund.

Qualified educational expenses are: tuition, fees, books, equipment, tutoring, special services, room and board. If Fuller forgoes college for one year to do missionary work in Luxembourg and raids his fund for travel expenses, he will be subject to tax on the appreciation of the fund plus a 10% penalty. Fuller must use his EIRA money within 30 days after he turns age 30 or be subject to the capital gains tax plus a 10% punishment.

Fuller can rollover his EIRA to a member of his family. Fuller can transfer these funds to his ten year old nephew Woolgar. Uncle Neville's contributions are not tax deductible. Fuller is the owner of the assets in his EIRA and this may prevent or limit his ability to receive financial aid. The Hope Credit or Lifetime Learning Credit will not be available if you use money from your IRA in a given year.

A Section 529 plan pays for approved higher educational expenses. The dispersals are federal tax free and cover the same expenses as the EIRA. Maximum contributions and terms vary state to state. Check your state to find the specifics of the plan. Unlike the EIRA there are no AGI or age limitations. The donor is the owner of the account and controls when distributions are made. Funds can be used for an accredited higher education institution in the U.S. and abroad.

Dawn Labarre creates a 529 for Hannah, the daughter of Duncan Lamble. Hannah marries Carlos Fuqua and devotes her time to her family. Dawn deletes Hannah as beneficiary of the 529 and names her first son Egbert as beneficiary. Dawn needs cash and bumps Egbert off the 529 and cashes in the checks. She will pay ordinary income tax on the gains plus 10% damages unless she uses the money for approved higher education expenses.

You can transfer assets from the EIRA to a 529. Your donation is considered a gift to the named beneficiary for gift tax purposes but qualifies for the annual $11,000 gift tax exclusion. You can front-load $55,000 (five years donations) reducing your estate tax liability. Remember, although the asset has left your estate, you the owner, maintain stewardship. 529s are inhabited by mutual funds that can be changed yearly; refer to the program details.

You may have an EIRA and a 529 for the same named beneficiary.

Suggestion: fully fund your retirement and your spouse's before another person's educational requirements. It is not likely in retirement you can rely on Hannah."

Money is not a real thing, but a means of exchanging real things. (G. D.H. Cole)

11

PHOTONS

Socrates meanders to the Village Square and notes Mogford Oxenham in front of the candle shop.

"Greetings, Mogford."

"I have shekels saved that I want to put to work. Sahib, please teach me."

"Investing is centered on risk and rewards. Your propagations are income and capital gains less capital destruction."

"What kind of remuneration can I await?"

"Anticipated rewards are based on historical results of similar investments. Corporate bonds have rendered between 6 to 7%. There is no warranty the future will repeat because it is unstable."

"How does instability affect my shekels?"

"The longer you wait to get paid, the greater the uncertainty. As the unforeseeability dilates, its kin (risk) escalates."

"I see. I see. Time and risk travel the same path. What else?"

"There are stakes that pay dividends. The larger the income component of the investment, the less risk because you receive money post haste. The fiscal capacity of the enterprise affects the consistency and quality of dividends paid."

"Please slow down, Sahib. Please tell me in another way."

"Filthy McSwain's Inc. makes hamburgers that many people love and has recorded increasing sales and proceeds for 20 years. Do you believe that Filthy will continue to do well?"

"Yes. I, my wife, the scant Mogfords, will raise our consumption of Mr. McSwain's burgers each year."

"Filthy McSwain's Inc. has durable and high-quality dividends."

"Mr. Socrates, please tell me more about risk."

"These are the main categories of risk. Business and industry risk: revenue/ profit could decline, bankruptcy, and the industry could be orphaned. Inflation risk: inflation rates will impact your pay off with bonds incurring greater erosion than shares. Market risk: in a broad decline stocks will lose value independent of company operations, and bond values will fall when interest rates climb. Liquidity risk: if a stow or bond is not actively traded, pricing will not be competitive."

"Hmm, if I want more than guaranteed compensation, I must get in bed with uncertainty."

"Since the market began crops have averaged annual returns of 10 to 11%, bonds 6 to 7%, short term T-bills 4.5%. Mogford, my humble student, your homework is to balance your goals with your risk menu."

"I need to know more about risk."

"If you buy one security, your entire return will rest on its performance. Regardless of the quality of this security, this is a high-risk approach. If you include nine other securities, of equal investment with dissimilar characteristics, you will spread and reduce your risk."

"Please tell me the bloodlines of time and risk."

"Ample time is critical to avoid exiting a security at an inopportune moment. Volatile materiels are treacherous because of their rocketing stub movements. If you sell in a gale, you may incur a large shrinkage. Do not buy volatile stocks unless you can supply sufficient slack and endure severe monetary changes. Fixed income investments are less volatile but can be buffeted by strong interest rate moves."

"What about timing risk?"

"If you have a large sum of shekels, put part of it to work monthly on a consistent basis. This will average out your deposits reducing the chance of buying the top of the market."

"I need help to sketch my investment portrait."

"These are the quadrants of the painting. Your risk endurance; foremost, you should be emotionally comfortable with the level of risk you assume. If discomfort exists, you are doomed because you will be ripe for errors. Do you remember when Osama Cum Laude destroyed the Cave Town Trade Center with Pterodactyls? The textile market closed more than one week and when it opened it disintegrated. Extreme emotional turmoil creates the quicksand of errors. If you sold during the meltdown, you received the short end. The market recovered and marched upward after the particles stabilized. Let's look at a one year interval.

People with a low acceptance of risk can handle losses of no more than 5% (money market funds, CDs, short-term bonds) annually. Investors with a moderate temperature can withstand retreats of 6–15% (long-term bonds, blue-chip or dividend paying fruit). Adventurers with the killer instinct can endure devastations over 15%(equities in the fields of technology, biotechnology, communications, small caps, emerging markets).

How do you balance income and betterment? If you rely on your portfolio to provide a meaningful part of your income, it is wise to seek securities that provide satisfactory proceeds that are steadfast with safety of principal (mortgage-backed bonds, AAA corporate bonds, A rated preferreds). If you are funding future expenses (retirement), securities that emphasize progress (common produce and REIT) are your ticket. Within the categories of income/growth there are many gradations enabling you to customize your security chest.

How much time do I have? Time is amiable or warlike. If you are young, decades lay before you. Early errors can be overcome. The passage of time reduces the wrinkles of risk. After you round 50, the investment clock winds down. Blunders may not be overcome and time compresses.

How soon do you need the money? To be in equities you need a minimum of five to ten years to level out stock market cycles. If it is one to five years you belong in the fixed income section that can be a blend of high-quality short, intermediate, or long bonds.

What are the tax implications? If you are fortunate to pay large amounts of tax put high income/growth securities in an IRA (securities traded for short-term gains belong here) since taxes are deferred. Tax exempt municipal bonds may be sensible. If your tax rate is at a lower rung of the ladder, high dividend deeds and REIT are appropriate."

"Please tell me adviser, how does aging effect my investing?"

"Quien Sabe. How long you count on to live? Do you have sufficient income to support your desired lifestyle? How has your appetite for risk evolved? Do you wish to bequeath a portion of your wealth? How long do you want to work? As the circumstance of one's life changes, the benefit/risk question pops up. Are you content with your holdings?"

"You are asking me to continuously examine my soul. OK, Sahib."

"We have to talk about how you construct your edifice of assets."

"Do you object if I eat a McSwain burger? Would you like one?"

"A Filthy, no thank you. You can invest in bolts, bonds or cash (money markets and short term CDs). Diversify within each class to temper risk. If you agonize over which resource to buy, Chariot Manufacturing Inc. or Pterodactyl Airlines, within a portfolio of 20 horses, the decision is muted. The failure of one pony in 20 will not be devastating."

"How do I decide how much of each stake to buy?"

"My dear friend, you must revisit your risk temperature, how much time before you cash out, squaring off income and augmentation. Between 1946 through 1991 *(after inflation)* stocks had an average annual score of 7.3%, bonds 1.3% (data from the S&P 500). One year holding periods reflect stows having a best grade of 52.6% and worst of -26.5%, bonds 29.1% and -1.3%. For ten years intervals vendibles best returns are 20.1% and worst 1.2%, bonds 13.1% and 1.3%. For 20 years we find 14.9% best gain for stocks and 6.5% worst, 9.4% and 2.2% for bonds."

"Voila. I see the beauty of time inventory. If I have time, it is a desirable houseguest. If I picked one year to invest in shares I could have lost more than half of my shekels and if I bought solely bonds, the victuals would have been nibbled by inflation. The recipe must include stocks and bonds and the concoction should be able to simmer."

"Although revenue may be your primary goal, it need not relegate you to fixed income alone. Subject to the size of your account and risk tolerance you can own high dividend paying utensils or REIT. If you need cash, you can sell part of the trusts."

"How do I mitigate stock market risk?"

"Locate core holdings that have exhibited consistent attainment over time (dividend paying deeds with developing potential). Surround these assets with a sprinkling of unrelated securities (small-cap, mid-cap, micro-cap, energy, healthcare, foreign, international, technology, biotechnology)."

"What do you think of the mini-mouse nest eggs?"

"They have done near 10% more than the S&P 500 stocks. I believe part of your money should be in micro-cap and small-caps. These investments exhibit greater risk, volatility, and uncertainty compared to the S&P 500 members. You need five to ten years for the diminutive end of the market. The challenges of this sector are: monies stay in the business and are not paid in dividends, there is less information available making research problematic, market value fluctuations can be precipitous and extreme, firms can be adversely affected by economic setbacks, access to capital and credit may be limited, larger competitors can muscle them out of the market because of their greater resources of capital, research, development, management, small companies may not be actively traded, less competition amongst buyers and sellers results in noncompetitive pricing."

"Foreign produce frighten me. Should I own them?"

"5 to 10% of your money can go overseas to aid diversification. Foreign exchange markets do not correlate with the U.S. market. Australia is a good example. Markets in developing countries offer opportunities that present large risk. Do not participate unless you bring your crash helmet. It is OK to allot a small amount of your cash to a well-reasoned speculative embryo. Fortune may bless you."

"Anything else?"

"Yes. Foreign trades incur currency risk (the currency may be devalued as respects the U.S. dollar) and country risk (political agitation may effect the economy)."

"Help me Sahib, an idea how I can diversify for income."

"High-yield bonds historically averaged 9 to 10% and that is similar to stocks. Part of your bond account can go high-yield but notice high-yield equates to high-risk. These bonds respond opposite to investment grade bonds. When interest rates are low it means business is stagnant and junk bonds face a greater default possibility (investment grade bonds appreciate in a low interest environment). When interest rates rise it means strong demand in a growing economy that benefits junk bonds because they are making money to pay the interest (high quality bonds will depreciate in a rising interest rate climate). You do not receive the sought after higher prize on high-yield bonds for free. The trade off is an abundance of volatility compared to high-grade bonds. If the admission is worth it, see the movie."

"Honorable mentor, I am growing weary. I would like the ideas of professional management without the cost of Mapower Kneebone. Is there another way?"

"Newsletters. Be aware of short term performance. If on January 1, 1991 you picked the newsletter with the best previous 12-month performance and continued this for each January through mid 1999 you would've had an annualized loss of 36.6% while the broad market (Wilshire 5000 index) gained 18.4% yearly."[1]

"Hmm, hero to hobo in 12 months."

"Let's follow the same design using five year trailing performance records. By following the leaders from January 1' 1991, through June 30, 1999, we would have garnered of 18.2% annually. If we use ten year intervals the score was 21.6%."

"Bingo"

"It is not as simple as you think. By abiding by the selections of a newsletter with the best previous ten year performance you will incur greater volatility than the Wilshire 5000 index. Your tax bite will be bigger. On a *risk adjusted* basis the index was the good show."

"I saw an analyst, Augar Cockermouth, on the telly this morning. Augar follows a stock called Moon Microsystems (MMS). He has advised the clients of his brokerage firm to buy MMS when he began coverage in 1996 ($7) continuously through April 2002 ($7). The rocket peaked at over $60 in 1999. If I began buying the pledge in 1996 and continued buying until April 2002 (this was Cockermouth's recommendation), my unrealized casualty would be staggering. What is the rationale for buying a stub at $7, $20, $40, $62, $35, $21, $15, $7 and never selling?"

"My dear tenderfoot, Augar Cockermouth produces good research about MMS that details the financial condition of the company and its profit prospects. Augar believes he knows what the value of the plant is, and what its budding value will be. He was right in 1996 when he said to buy MMS at $7, in 1997 at $10, in 1998 at $13, in 1999 at $20, in 2000 at $41. He was wrong in 2001 at 60 $ and 2002 at $10. The Soothsayers Society believes their job is to create market targets based on their research. Cockermouth would declare Filthy McSwain's Inc. is a strong buy (currently $20) with a twelve month target of $30. Augar is a soothsayer who did his undergraduate work at Alchemy Institute and received a doctorate from Delphic University."

"Hold it. Hold it. Hold it. I met Gasport Earnshaw at a Hindu Brotherhood breakfast and he introduced himself as a farmer from the same firm as Dr. Cockermouth. What relationship does Gasport have with Cockermouth?"

"Cockermouth is paid $15 million a year to write research reports based on his visions or dreams to rally the foot soldiers."

"On the boardwalk in Atlantic City, I paid Maleva the gypsy woman, $5 to read my hoof. How is Cockermouth different than Maleva?"

"There may be no difference. We know Cockermouth has studied economics, finance, and alchemy and holds a doctorate from Delphic University."

"Sahib, is Cockermouth worth $15 million based on his research, his ability to divine, or his cheerleading?"

"My devoted apprentice, for less than $500,000.one can obtain an outstanding professor of business and finance to write reports. Maleva has invested in the Wilshire 5000 index that means her long term performance far surpasses Cockermouth's. You can retain Maleva for less than $100,000 dollars a year. Augar's purpose is to get Gasport excited about selling seeds."

"Hmm, Dr. Cockermouth is a well-paid cheerleader. What else?"

"Luton O'Greedy is an investment banker for the firm. He helps raise money for companies through offerings of carrots. The firm is paid handsome fees for Luton's service. It is rare for Cockermouth to impugn a stock if Luton is attempting to raise money for that firm; Augar will suture his lips."

"This is getting too complicated."

"A fortune in fees is being paid by Pterodactyl Airlines to Luton O'Greedy to sell 1,000,000 new shares at 15 to $20. While at a séance, Augar has a vision that the annelid worm, Pterodactyl fuel supply, is threatened. Augar has a $22 destination for the crop and decides to revise it to $8. If Cockermouth publishes his revised report Luton's deal will collapse and the firm will lose a robust payday. Augar believes his visions are reliable but decides to shuck this one. Luton does his deal and the 1,000,000 clams are sold at $20, pleasing everyone. Augar attends a different séance."

"I sense there is more to this story."

"If an initial public offering (IPO) is done in a favorable market climate, the price of the plume will rise the first day of trading and continue to rise until it finds its plateau. If Luton O'Greedy is bringing out Pterodactyl Airlines in an IPO, and you are a client of Gasport, you may be able to buy the shares. Gasport will explain to you there is a great amount of interest in the stock and it should do well. He will say that you are not presumed to sell the fruitage within six months to cash in your winnings. If you do sell, you will be shut out of all IPOs."

"This is most confusing Sahib. Why must I hold the stock when I want to sell?"

"Luton O'Greedy has a good relationship with the management of Pterodactyl Airlines. They are pleased he raised $20 million for them and Luton's firm exposed their teeth when they saw the $1.4 million check for services furnished. The firm desires to be in good standing with Pterodactyl to be called for new business. The loftier the exchange cost of Pterodactyl, the greater the fondness management has for Luton's firm. When Gasport tells you not to sell, you are helping to support the stub."

"I see those exciting commercials on the telly showing attractive people scampering about to the aid of investors. A somber voice intones, "We treat each investor, one at a time". Is this untruth?"

"Earnshaw's firm pours millions into the telly. Do you believe these expenditures are for your benefit?"

"Should I not buy Pterodactyl Airlines if I am warned not to sell it within six months? Do I disregard the valuable research of Dr. Augar Cockermouth?"

"No. Be observant if conflicts of interest exist. If Augar recommends you buy a bolt, ask if O'Greedy is doing the investment banking for this equity. If such a relationship exists, you have been forewarned."

"I see. I see. I see. I was wondering why few prophets advise you to sell a stock. The analyst firm may have had or may anticipate doing investment banking business with the company. If Dr. Cockermouth is unkind to a company, his firm will be scratched from the list of potential investment bankers."

"Yes my conscript, it is helpful to have a picture of the feeding chain in the securities industry: the firm, the executives, Luton O'Greedy, Augar Cockermouth, Gasport Earnshaw, the shareholders, the client."

"There is another member of the party?"

"Yes there is Rory Scales, the corporate accountant (CPA). The American Institute of Certified Public Accountants (AICPA) is a potent lobby in Scrubbington. They have been successful in blocking legislation against their interest."

"What do you mean?"

"The AICPA is a society that promulgates the rules of financial reporting and its oversight. The larger accounting firms fund it and its role is to protect their interest. The accounting firm, Mcgufficke Co., audits the books of Filthy McSwain's. Every three months Filthy reports earnings results derived from the audit of Mcgufficke. Mcgufficke offers golf and tennis consultation to the executives of McSwain. The consultation work is the most bounteous part of the accounting business."

"Hold it. What do measuring financial results have to do with consultation?"

"Nothing. Mcgufficke is revenue driven, and if they can pick up cushy dollars by shortening a handicap or improving a backhand, they will."

"I'm confused. What does footwork in tennis have to do with a quarterly report?"

"Escarole."

"Hmm. I see. You speak in riddles because you want me to think. You are suggesting that the financial reporting may not be objective because of the lucrative golf and tennis franchise."

"Generally Acceptable Accounting Practices (GAAP) are the rules and regulations that govern financial reporting. These procedures were created by and are interpreted by the accounting industry. Numerous situations occur where judgment is the arbiter."

"OK. You are suggesting the honorable firm of Mcgufficke will compromise their audit to favor McSwain because of the cozy consultation work?"

"Yes, my trainee, items come up which can be glossed over, interpretations can swing positive or negative, warning post can be covered."

"Godfrey Daniel. Does Mcgufficke misrepresent?"

"I do not know. I believe the golf and tennis fees will redouble the probability. It is best to be aware of all the forces at work. Do not believe what you read, hear, see. *Observe. Analyze. Respond.*"

"Go home my friend and be back tomorrow, we will talk about you."

12

BEHAVIORAL FINANCE

"You look haggard. Did you sleep well?"

"No, Sahib. We covered many troubling topics yesterday. You have called into question the pillars of capitalism: Dr. Augar Cockermouth, Luton O'Greedy, Cornelius Card, and Gasport Earnshaw."

"If I have not made sound argument, reject my thoughts. If you choose to believe otherwise, support your observation with fact and steeled reasoning."

"No. It is a different issue. My talks with you bring me to self-education and independence. Please continue."

"What do you think determines the cost of a carrot?"

"What a buyer and seller agreed to."

"True. Moreover, the perception of what the buyer thinks the crop is worth. The perception of the buyer is how he sees the territory but the territory may not be the map (reality). The buyer falls into the pit where he finds Cockermouth because he, like Augar, believes he can see tomorrow. The projected value of a stake is a moving particle; you have a gain one moment and a downfall the next. Your judgment about buying the article will be incomplete and imperfect. Since Augar will not tell you when to sell, you are an orphan at peril."

"Are you suggesting there are many facets to the pricing of a stock?"

"Research regarding deed valuations for the period of 1982 to 1997 recorded when it was sunny in Manhattan, stocks had an average annual gain of 25%, and without sun the gain was 8%."

"Are you telling me reserves rise with the sun?"

"No, there is more to the cake than the frosting."

"What do you make of a high stock value follow by a crash?"

"Yes. Gaggle behavior. Investors climb aboard a movement, oblivious to the hazards. A common mistake is buying last year's feverish mutual fund and it incinerates the following year. A more lethal error is overconfidence. When your investments are marching forward briskly, you believe you have the sorcerer's touch and jeopardy will not accompany you."

"You are leading me to believe emotion is fertile in the market."

"We are emotional beings. Behavior is driven by feelings. Decisions are guided by passion."

"I am a chemical engineer by careful thought, not emotion."

"What did you feel when you chose this field?"

"I was excited. My research process is without emotion."

"Do you experience passion during research?"

"Yes. Human behavior, by definition is emotional."

"How would you measure the magnitude of emotion in money, politics, and religion?"

"I believe it is enormous."

"It has been thought that people make financial decisions based on rational thought."

"But master, emotion will be part of the thinking, and it must follow rationality will be compromised."

"Stressed with uncertainty, rationality is diluted, inconsistencies pop up and competency is assailed. Research has shown people hang onto their losing securities while selling their winners. Often the winners that were sold outperformed, for several months, the losers that were retained."[2]

"Hmm, I don't understand. Isn't it true you get a tax deduction for a realized capital fatality? And this tax deduction has dollar value?"

"Yes."

"Why would one pay tax on a capital gain where it could be offset with a capital loss?"

"Dear pupil, when a person considers selling a losing security it stimulates many emotions. People feel more pain with a loss than elation with a gain. The pain associated with the sale of a losing resource may inhibit the person from pushing the ejection button. Acceptance of responsibility for owning a miscalculation can leave a bitter residue. Few are comfortable with embracing the negative effects of responsibility. One may have to grapple with that this is a repeat of a similar error that can prompt a stinging question. Why the replay? Other acid memories can surface. Why did I watch this tomato decay? I should have sold it last year. I was sure it would come back. I invest for the long term as proposed by Gasport. It's Earnshaw's fault. I don't feel comfortable about selling. The last time I sold a flop it became a charming prince. I feel lousy and don't know what to do with the money. Everyone else is doing poorly."

"The investor is hampered in the buying process because of the thousands of stocks and mutual funds available. Studies have shown that individual investors buy ordinance that have sparked their attention. Extreme sales volume increases and large tag movements (positive or negative) breed investor activity. A news story covered on the telly bloated the volume of the projectile fivefold that day. Pay outs on securities purchased because of news or swelled volumes have not done better than the market, nor have they done better than the articles sold."

"Sahib, again, there is no silver bullet."

"Investors are prone to underreaction and overreaction and the timing is off. When you respond quickly to a situation, emotion may be the principal driver. When you do not address a state of affairs, the ostrich effect may be at play. Before you react or ignore, analyze the relevant factors."

"Hmm, this is tricky stuff, to avoid under or overreacting. One has to sort out and apply pressing information."

"People partition money into sectors. Money is money and its use should be focused on your needs holistically. I will be conservative in funding retirement, but the unexpected $1,000 bonus I received can buy a speculative stake, and if the investment is a washout I haven't lost anything. Nonsense. You have lost $1,000 and the purchasing power that it represents. People that have unrealized withdrawals in a brokerage account state that their disappointments are on paper. Poppycock. The losses are real because you have lost buying power."

"What is gone is gone."

"Anchoring has cost many a penny to an investor. Anchoring occurs when former values are used to predict coming value. If the stock sold for $20 and now sells for $5, the investor believes it is a steal at $5. Before pouncing on the deal, one should examine the reasons it is $5 and its prospects for sprouting. Studies have reported that an anchor in place does not move much, and the investor is not likely to cut the line. This lays the seeds for underreaction and failure to account for new information that may signal a turning point. Perhaps, one should buy it at $5 and not because it is $5.

Overreaction occurs when people believe they see a trend and that the trend will self-perpetuate. At one time growth crops do well, and at a different time value stocks do well, if we look over ten year periods we will find they are similar in merit.

People believe they see patterns and the patterns will continue. Research reflects in coin toss experiments, most people believe that a sequence of heads/tails/heads/tails/heads will occur more than that all heads, all tails, or a different order. The probability of each of these results is equal. Investors see order where there is none and believe randomness is a quirk.

The concept of trends is anchored and the unknown destiny is disregarded. Augar Cockermouth predicts a quarterly s report will be $1 and the result is $1.25. Augar believes he is right and the company is wrong. For the next report Augar will stay closer to the $1 he originally predicted because of anchoring."

"Yes master, anchors belong in the sea, not in my portfolio."

"The greatest toxicity in investing behavior lies in overconfidence. Similar to high blood pressure, the patient is unaware of the disease that is a silent slayer. In 1998 and 1999 people were asked to assume that they had an account that held Internet studs within average value of $100 per share. What did they believed the intrinsic value was? They responded $50 per share. They were asked what you think will happen to the appraisals over the next six months? They believed the judgments would be higher and they would know when to sell before a price decline."[3]

"They thought the tags of the Internet bolts was inflated but would continue to rise. They had uncovered a trend and could predict its reversal. This was a group of special people."

"Eager student, these folks were overconfident and manufactured their reality. Studies have recorded that people believe they are better than average drivers, they are not as likely to lose their jobs as their peers, and they will avoid a heart attack."

"Negative occurrences happen to other people, not me."

"Numerous experiments point up people are overconfident about the exactness of their knowledge. When an investor is inexperienced and successful, overconfidence takes root. He believes his good returns are a function of his abilities. As he gathers greater experience, his assessment of his skills diminishes. Overconfidence cultivates inflated trading activity while lack of confidence reduces this activity."

"Is Dr. Cockermouth overconfident?"

"Research has declared that when stock chefs are 80% sure a brew will rise, they are correct about 40% of the time."

"Maleva or Cockermouth? I understand Dr. Cockermouth took his Ph.D. at Delphic University, but I must question the quality of his education. Where did he graduate in his class? How does he conjure his visions? Does he use dream analysis? Does he, Luton O'Greedy, Gasport Earnshaw meet for séances?"

"Excessive trading will devour your assets. In a large study covering 1991 to 1996, the most frequently traded accounts posted an annual score of 11.4%

while the less actively traded accounts produced 16.4% (the S&P 500 netted 17.9%). Overconfidence stimulates excessive trading that depletes wealth."

"Oh my, one must trade guardedly and selectively. I read a curious article that said that people prefer to bet on the toss of a coin before is tossed. Is this the Augar effect? I held the impression that people made investment decisions on fact and logic while I find idiosyncratic behavior is plentiful."

"Dear novice, we anthropomorphize our relationship with a stock. You buy and it rises. Most people would assign an acceptable rating of 1. You buy a stock and its worth declines. The rating would be -1. The produce you bought rises followed by a decline. The rating is -2. Your merchandise falls, recovers, and posts a gain. The rating is +2. The investor is tying his emotions and a grading system to the travels of a trust. One feels better about a gain in an asset that had a reversal as opposed to a gain in a reserve that began a winner and did not become unworthy. The output of the two stocks is identical. The emotions linked to each security are different. It follows that many investors feel worse about an article that starts out favorably, but relinquish its gains and became a loser.

My dear friend Mogford, if you accept this, deep and troubling insights emerge. People who sell equities with a gain because of a decrease in the worth will feel worse than if they had held it and the market carried it higher. Investors will retain losers because they will feel better if the stake turns around and appreciates whereas if the equity continues to lose value, the pain will be muted. If a person has a position at a loss and the paper reaches the break even point, he will sell it because if it retreats in retail, he will feel worse than if it rises in value."

"I heed your counsel; I must segregate my emotions from my investment behavior."

"Yes. What we have been discussing may answer the question that has bedeviled investors. Why do they sell winners too soon and hold onto losers too long?"

"Tell me more about the torment of second thoughts. I believe this has hobbled me."

"This may go to the hub of why people resist unloading poor performing resources. Denial. The torture one feels confronting failure. Wares are best bought, sold, or retained based on their presumed prospects, not pain or pleasure. Pain will cause you to keep your pistol holstered. Pleasure will lubricate your trigger finger."

"Let's go back to why people sell their winners and maintain the mongrels."

"Research has uncovered that: people shun risk when they consider the possibility of a gain; people assume risk when confronted with the possibility of demise."[4]

"Yes I have spent costly time there. I have sold desirable stocks because of my fear of losing the gains. I have stored plants in purgatory assuming the risk of their sins."

"Investor A holds the mutual fund of Cornelius Card and considers switching to Mapower Kneebone but takes no action. Investor B moves from Kneebone to Card. Mapower produces the best harvest for the year. Which investor is more upset? Each person had the same gain."

"I'll take investor B."

"Correct. How did you arrive at your choice?"

"People grieve action more than inaction. If I act, I will have to live with the outcome. If I do nothing, I can bury the situation and that provides comfort as opposed to distress."

"Research finds people systematically place pygmy weight on particular types of information while according other kinds of information greater importance."[5]

"Aha. The same information is interpreted in different ways. People see what they want to see, and how they interpret events is skewed by their prejudice."

"Let's go back to overconfidence and its effect on exorbitant trading. Relying on data for over 35,000 accounts we find that men trade 45% more than woman and have 1.4% lower risk adjusted payments. Single men trade 67% more than single woman with 2.3% lower grades."[6]

"Overconfidence spurs trading and brings inferior results. Sahib, too much activity is no good, nor is hanging on to sagging stalks. It does strike one's mettle to find a balance."

"It is the inner game you must master. Do not fall prey to overconfidence. Do not permit your emotions to set you up for failure. *When the emotion comes cloaked in excitement, fallback, analyze. Act based on your clearest judgment.*"

"Please recommend books that may be helpful."

"Barron's Dictionary of Finance and Investment Terms by John Downes and Jordan Elliot Goodman.495 pages, $9.95 How to Read a Financial Report by John A. Tracy. A Beginner's Book in Understanding Financial Reports. $14.95 The Illustrated Real Estate Dictionary by Michael C.Thomsett. 245 pages, $12.95"

13

THE CONFESSION BOOTH

"O Sahib, I wish we could have had these talks before I started investing."

"What do you mean?"

"My first debacle occurred during the Gulf War. I relied on the belief that wars upset produce markets. I thought the Gulf War would drag on the way the Viet Nam war did, and U.S. casualties would accrue. We would win the war, but not without a good amount of lives lost with negative domestic political and economic effects. I sold every security in my account before the war began."

"Were you upset when you made the decision to sell?"

"Yes, I was agitated. Now I understand emotion should not steer financial decisions."

"Did you stay out of the market?"

"I was sure the market would tank because of the impending conflict and I bought an index put option for $10,000."

"And?"

"My brilliance was quickly rewarded; the option was worth $20,000 in one week. I was a genius investor. I had sidestepped the downturn in the market and was about to cash in as a result of the coming carnage. I saw my option being worth 70 to $100,000 with the onset of the war. I had a brief thought of selling the option and grabbing the quick $10,000 boost, but I spoke to myself saying: "why settle for a small slice of the pie, I have outmaneuvered them and it is my time to expand my winnings"."

"What happened?"

"The value of the option began to decline, the war broke out, and in 90 days the option had zero value."

"A number of key emotional/psychological forces came to bear in your story. Can you tell me what they are?"

"I made the assumption I could read the forthcoming. I predicted the course of the war and the effects on the market. I believed I was one of the few people who could see what was about to happen. My knowledge was secret. When the option doubled in value I was not full. I could clearly see the value continue to climb."

"Stop. What was at work?"

"Overconfidence, I could not accept my suppositions would fail."

"When the value of the option went to $10,000 you were even. Why did you not sell?"

"I felt I lost $10,000."

"You were even. Did you believe you made the wrong decision not to sell a $20,000?"

"I would be admitting I made a mistake. I would have to face the damage of my greed was $10,000. I believed the value of the option would rise."

"What made you believe this?"

"The negative effects the war would bring to the market."

"When the value of the index option dropped below $10,000, did you consider you were wrong and should sell?"

"No. I could not bear the pain of being wrong. This pain was worse than loss of money. I would prefer to stay with my conviction and risk total failure. Not selling was less painful than selling."

"And when the option was valueless?"

"I felt stupid and wiped away the episode unaware of the psychological dynamics at play."

"Do you mean you learned nothing?"

"Yes."

"Why?"

"I believe the learning would have beckoned pain that I wanted to cover."

"Pain is a warning. Be it physical or mental. Your body is saying pay attention."

"I took out a home equity loan of $15,000 for 6.75% interest. I use the proceeds to buy a mutual fund that owned dividend paying assets. My goal was to outpace the 6.75% interest rate without assuming a great deal of risk."

"Excellent. That was a well thought out approach. What happened?"

"My fund stagnated while the market produced potent gains for technology, communications and aggressive growth mutual funds."

"And?"

"I sold my fund and bought the funds that were advancing."

"Stop. What did your behavior say?"

"I saw a flow that I believed would continue, and I would have the knowledge when to sell."

"And?"

"My account was handsome. In one and half years my holdings were $25,000 while my former fund would have been $17,000."

"And?"

"Today my account is worth $5,000 and my former fund would be worth $24,000."

"What did you think when your funds swooned?"

"I thought it was temporary and that they would regain their former heights."

"What was this believe supported by?"

"A warm summer breeze."

"During the time your funds were rising, how long did you think this would occur?"

"My excitement told me forever."

"Why did you abandon the first fund?"

"Greed. Passion."

"What did you take from this experience?"

"I should not permit greed to redirect a sound plan. Streaks do occur. The information you receive is historical, it is similar to reading exchequer markers in a newspaper. No one can predict the life span of a trend."

"Why did you not sell when your funds were worth $25,000?"

"Avarice. I could see my fortune growing. Overconfidence. It was clear my wealth was multiplying."

"As with the option, when your mutual funds turned south you were unable to sell. Why?"

"Pain hobbles."

"Greed and overconfidence prohibited you from selling both the option and the mutual fund when they produced sizable gains. Pain froze your fingers to selling when these investments dissolved. Is there more?"

"Oh yes, Sahib, my story chest is full. In 1998 Internet pledges glowed and I owned NetBank that I bought for $5 a share, and sold for $20 in four months.1998 and 1999 was the halcyon days of Internet markers. New Internet seeds would start trading their first day at $20 and close at $80. Many of these vouchers surpassed a hundred dollars a share in the first few months of trading. These companies raised billions. Nine months after I sold NetBank it reached $250 a share."

"Other than your unfortunate timing, what did this tell you?"

"I misunderstood the nature of Internet equities, their extreme volatility.

The cell split three for one in 1999 and maintained its lofty tag until the fall of 1999. I scraped the crumbs off the table while leaving the loaf of bread. I learned when you buy a speculative issue you must give it room to run on the range. If you buy a race horse you should allow it to do what it does best, sprint. I cannot tell you I would have sold at the maximum. It would have been higher than $20 a share, and if I had not sold the split adjusted merit today is about $48 a share."

"And?"

"I am the same as the people in the studies we spoke about. I like to think about myself as being smarter than other investors although my behavior contradicts this. The folks in the experiments sold their winners too soon as I did with NetBank, and caressed their losers until paralysis, as I did with the mutual funds."

"What happened next?"

"I am pleased to say the dummy can learn. I bought Active Apparel in December 1997 at $2.20 per share and sold it one year later at $17.70 per share. This company is a sportswear manufacturer. During this time, if your company put out a press release indicating you had an Internet strategy, your ordinance would catapult. One night while making love to Ms. Oxenham, I heard from a news report Active Apparel went from $5 a share to $25 (closed at $20) because they announced the inception of a website. There was no rational reason for the rapid rise in dues."

"Excellent. What lessons did you heed?"

"I held Active Apparel, a speculative property, permitting it to pop. I could have sold at $5 a share for over a 100% reward. When the ticker exploded for a nonsensical reason, I cashed out. I did not repeat the error of NetBank."

"There is light. What happened next?"

"Do you remember the communications mutual funds I told you I bought?"

"Yes"

"I compounded my ineptitude by buying WorldCom and AT&T close to their highs."

"Why?"

"I was sure the telecommunications industry was a certified money producer."

"Did you study the eggs and their industry?"

"No. My decision was based on my fondness for their industry."

"Do you think you were dating a lovely young lady?"

"That is the way I behaved. The lady turned into a corpse. Oversupply, overcapacity, and competition overwhelmed this industry."

"And?"

"I have heard you speak unkind words about Dr. Augar Cockermouth. The independent analysts at Standard and Poor's have shortcomings. They recommended Covad Communications, a firm that installed digital subscriber lines that provide instant access to the Internet. Standard and Poor's touted the strong output potential when it was $45. I waited to buy it at $18. Today is under $2."

"When the tag went from $45 to $18, did you investigate the reasons?"

"No. Standard and Poor's continued their buy recommendation.

I see I must give more credence to what is happening in the market as opposed to seers' suggestions."

"What other analysts' recommendations have you bought?"

"Dr. Cockermouth said to buy Canadian Pacific because it was being broken into four companies that had a composite value of $85 per share. I bought the shares at $42 and waited for my bounty. When the company was divided it had a collective value of $34 per share. I sold the shares and had lunch with Maleva."

"What is the optimistic part of your story?"

"I was able to sell Canadian Pacific and move on without regret."

"Marvelous. Tell me a happy story."

"I was reading the financial news to find Immunex was hammered from $18 to $12 in one day on heavy volume. Immunex was testing its main drug (Embrel) to treat congestive heart failure. Embrel was on its way to becoming a billion dollar drug for a different disorder. I researched Immunex and found it to be sound financially with hearty prospects. I believe the downpour of selling was fuelled by hysteria, not by where the company was going. I bought at $12.10 and sold at $25.50 one year later."

"Wonderful."

"I must tell you about my shorting experience that uncovers the reverse side of overconfidence."

"What do you mean?"

"HomeStore.com was one of the wizards produced from the Internet froth. I read an article in a business magazine that questioned how the firm recognizes revenue. HomeStore.com sells advertising space to real estate brokers. The database of the Multiple Listing Service is incorporated. The homebuyer can review houses in the neighborhoods of interest via the Internet and be referred to a subscribing real estate broker. HomeStore.com offered other buying services associated with home ownership: moving, furniture, financing and interior decorating. The business model was to be a web-based supermarket of services and products to the home buyer. Revenue would flow from subscriptions paid by real estate brokers and advertising fees. I visited HomeStore's website to look for a house where I live in southern New Jersey. There were no listings. I thought the sheen on HomeStore was suspect if I couldn't find a house in an area that was growing.

On review of the trading behavior of HomeStore, I found it was a high-wire act; it was $100 and would move 10 to $20 in a day. I believed HomeStore's concept was attractive but had reservations it could produce the revenue being priced into the trove. I sold it short (an unowned stock is sold by borrowing it from the broker, and predicting the worth will decline enabling one to repurchase at a lower point resulting in a profit) building up a harvest of $9,000. I held a strong belief that HomeStore was a hollow company that would implode. In June of 2000 I sold short 400 shares of HomeStore at $32 a share. At this time Internet spaceships had been pummeled, and the market was continuing to punish them.

I observed HomeStore on a daily basis to ascertain if it was building a sustainable business machine. It was not. I was sure it would inflame leaving a residue. When one sells short the peril faced is the goods will appreciate, and will have to be repurchased at a higher price causing a misadventure. I accepted I could be wrong in my judgment about HomeStore, and desired to protect myself if its ticket rose. If the contract reached $50, I would buy back 400 shares and digest the mishap. Despite my powerful belief that it had no future value, I did not want the exposure of a larger debacle.

In August of 2000 the arrow hit $50, and I covered my short position, incurring a fee of $7,400 that scrubbed most of my winnings on the horse."

"Your stories become richer in complexity. Crosscurrents of logic/emotion collide. What did you sift from your HomeStore experience?"

"I will deal with that after I complete the short selling picture. Before I shorted HomeStore I had shorted Etoys, a retailer of toys on the net. I did not believe this company could reach viability, or if it did, it could justify its current value. I sold short a hundred shares at $20 and covered it within a week for a charge of $1,000. Amazon.com was shorted numerous times in the range of $60 to $75, $50, $30, $16. One short trade resulted in an impediment while the overall Amazon account had a plentiful profit. I did not believe Amazon was a likely candidate for bankruptcy court (I believed this for HomeStore and Etoys), but that its share value was grossly overstated."

"Tell me what you extracted from short selling."

"Whether you buy long or sell short, the devil is in your emotional response to gain/loss. Today Etoys is in Valhalla. I was perturbed when it moved quickly from $20 to $30. My business analysis that this was a company that would be challenged to survive the next few years had not changed. Market delirium spiked the rag, and out of panic I covered my position for a $1,000 lesson. I knew Etoys could move like a cheetah but was unwilling to provide it with sufficient room. If I am going to enter the jungle, I should be aware of the behavior of its inhabitants. I converted a successful trade into a deficit because of the foreboding of a flop. The dread became ruin."

"What is the inner tale of HomeStore?"

"Today HomeStore is a $2 stud. The fundamentals of the company were weak, as I had predicted. The SEC has investigated the company for fraudulent accounting practices and found exaggerated revenue reported resulting in a restatement of prior years. The year after I covered my short position HomeStore underwent a steady decline to $20. At the time I covered my short position, I was sure my bet against HomeStore was sound and rational. I did not want to risk further mishap and covered my position. The Etoys education was partial and did not end with a diploma. Cowardice bullied logic and reason whimpered away. Anxiety flipped a wealth creating trade to a substantial comeuppance."

"Did you graduate?"

"Yes. The tuition was expensive but tax-deductible. Amazon turns a different chapter. I made a succession of winning trades as the rag backslid. I thought the equity would become an $8 fabric, it did. I was absent from its long lowering because of closing my positions when I had a satisfactory net. I sacrificed potential long-term gains for short-term fortune. I wanted to seize the riches because I cringed they might vanish."

"What would you say is the dominant emotion in investor behavior?

"*Fear.*"

"What would the secondary emotion be?"

"Regret."

"Can you tie together your experiences of buying long and selling short?"

"When I retain securities that have a loss it is because I do not want to deal with the pain of accepting the bruise. Instead of analyzing the outlook of the investment and comparing with a different investment, I pray to Vishnu for assistance."

"What do you do with holdings that are satisfactory?"

"I will sell them, independent of their prognosis while holding onto my losers. I understand I will pay capital gains taxes, but I prefer to pay the tax rather than deal with the torment of a loss. I will call upon Brahman for help."

"Is there another topic?"

"Yes. When I buy long I am overconfident and maintain my optimistic outlook regardless of changing events. When I sell short I am not confident. If the sticker moves against me, despite my analysis indicating the stock price should decline, I protect my position."

"Why?"

"I grieve a greater deterioration."

"What is the interplay of overconfidence, underconfidence and fright?"

"My confidence has no effect on the value of a security. Apprehension does not impact the cost of the auto. To buy, sell or hold should be based on a conscientious analysis of its outlook. *The brothers and sisters of emotion should not gain admission.*"

14

MISDIRECTION

"Step right up. Step right up. Step right up. Come closer. This is your lucky day. My name is Eddy Roper and I have a proposition for you. Young man, you with the freckles, did you bring your lunch money?" A 12 year old farmer nods. "Good. I will show you how to get some of old man Roper's cash. What is your name?" The lad moves up to the table and whispers, "Fidelio." "Please observe we have three shells and one peanut. I put in the peanut under one shell and now watch my hands (Eddy rotates the shells in a semicircle).

OK, which shell has the peanut? Fidelio points to a shell that Eddy picks up to reveal the peanut. My, you are a sharpshooter. Fidelio's eyes shine and his cheeks broaden. All right, here is your chance to make an easy buck. I place the peanut under the shell. Now watch carefully. Roper shuffles the three shells. OK, Mr. Fidelio, place $1 in front of the shell that holds the peanut.

Eddy turns over a shell, empty. Godfrey Daniel, that's bad luck."

"Master, I want to manage my investments. My cupboard is full with spoiled vegetables. Emotion has been stripped from my paradigm. Although I remain error prone, my faults will diminish in number and severity. I accept my results are a reflection of me, not short-term external forces. Please help me pick materiels."

"Do not believe what you read. Do not believe what you see. Do not believe what you hear. *Observe. Analyze. Respond.*"

"Let's get started."

"A critical element of a company is the integrity and honesty of its management. Financial reporting is a driver of traffic prices. Executive salaries and benefits are linked to the firm's share value. This leads to pressure to maintain and up the tariff of the goods. Accounting is not a science and is subject to judgment and interpretation."

"You're giving me macro talk. Please make it micro talk."

"If a firm consistently reports attractive earnings unfolding, it translates to a higher sticker number. The monies may be real or imaginary"

"Why?"

"Puffing of earnings will occur when sales are registered too quickly. This is accomplished by: shipping goods before a deal is complete, logging revenue when vital questions are unanswered, and recording income when service remains to be performed."

"I must break the waterline to see what lies below."

"Companies may report income on the exchange of like assets. The firm exchanges property with the book value of $2,500 that has a market value of $10,000 and records a $7,500 imaginary gain. At times firms record refunds for returned merchandise as sales. Companies can report sales made to affiliates that are not arms length transactions."

"Learned instructor, is Eddy Roper in the executive suite?"

"Selling an undervalued asset can pump profits. A building with a book value of $10,000 is sold for $25,000. A company can pay off its debt reducing its interest expense and increasing its proceeds. One time gains may be included in operating income. An enterprise receives money for an out of court settlement. Firms might commingle nonrecurring gains with operating income that will overstate profits."

"Accounting gives me a headache."

"Sleigh of hand occurs when a company moves current expenses forward by classifying research and development cost as an asset rather than an expense. This overstates current year earnings and understates next year's results."

"I am befuddled. What is the purpose of shifting money?"

"A prime goal of a company is to produce consistent, climbing profits. If it has to borrow from future earnings to support current numbers, you will get the Eddy Roper effect."

"Do you mean I will not be able to tell which shell the peanut is under?'

"Yes. Another accounting stunt is burying liabilities. When an airline gives frequent flier miles to a customer they are deferring the cost of that trip. It is an unborn liability. The airline records the cash received that boost this year's revenue while ignoring the coming expense."

"Does one have to be a detective to interpret a financial report?"

"It helps. Another tactic is to delay current income, setting it aside in a piggy-bank, to act as a bailout account. A firm can create a reserve to postpone earnings. A tag price will respond more kindly, if it reflects earnings progress of 10%, 15%, 20% over three years rather than 30%, 15%, 0%. If the company attenuates the strong 30% earnings the first year and spreads it out over three years, the sticker is more likely to augment. When one borrows from the current to fund posterity, the company may be deferring calamity. In the above example, when the company had 0% earnings growth in the third year, this could be a symptom of serious internal problems that should be communicated to the shareholders. Income management distorts the true picture of the operating performance of the firm."

"Please continue with the legerdemain."

"A company may want to make next year's achievement greater by moving inevitable expenses to the present year. New management enters and wants to impress with a good report card. They accelerate depreciation that diminishes current year figures. Next year's earnings look good and they are heroes."

"I took a course in accounting in college and this reminds me of a joke that the teacher told us. A company was reviewing accountants to prepare financial reports. They presented data to three accountants posing the question how much federal income tax will be due? One CPA responded $1 million, the next answered $1.1 million and the last inquired how much do you want to pay?"

"Dear cadet, I read an article in the Bluff Street Journal about a software company. An in house investigation of the firm's accounting prompted a restatement increasing the debit for 2000, decreasing the loss for 1999 and contracting the earnings for 1998. The company was under scrutiny by the Securities Exchange Commission for bookkeeping irregularities. The firm was recording revenue for goods delivered into the distribution channel before they were finalized as customer sales, a practice called "stuffing the channel"."

"I see why the honesty of management is critical. A firm could choreograph a musical producing a good song and dance routine with surprise acts. Oh, Honorable Teacher, I am dissuaded from picking tickers. The demands of knowledge, experience, emotional intelligence and fortuity are foreboding. I could make good decisions that are polluted by moral frailty. I will buy index funds and save the angst."

15

SHADOWS

As Socrates does his chores in the Agora he meets Mogford's brother Bulmer in front of the arsenal.

"Hey, Bulmer, what's new?"

"I was talking to Mogford and he told me you put the willies into him about buying stocks. Is this true?"

"Mogford told me he was going to invest in index funds. This is a sound, straightforward approach. Tell me what the willies that you refer to are."

"Mogford is afraid to buy stocks."

"Mogford and I had a forthright discussion about the requirements to become a successful individual investor."

"Yes I know. You did not include courage as a necessary ingredient."

"I believe Mogford made a decision that was appropriate for him that would be beneficial for most investors. Sheath your sword and buy index funds."

"In my heart I know I'm right. I can beat the market. I see clearly without overconfidence. I will carry the colors of my fair lady forward."

"Many a knight has ridden into battle to incur casualty of limb or life."

"Without risk, without life."

"OK, we will begin with the execution of a field mouse.

The principals of finance and economics sustain the consciousness of the produce market. Entities of commerce have value relative to one another. The supermarket sells Turkish pasta for 40¢ a pound and Italian pasta $1.60. Wild rice is $1 a pound. Wild rice is less expensive than Italian pasta and more expensive than Turkish pasta. The chef at Filthy McSwain's restaurant earns $10 per hour while Mapower Kneebone, makes $300 per hour. Society places relative value on the goods and services it produces. 1 U.S. dollar is worth 1.5 Canadian dollars. I want you to develop the habit of thinking of an investment dollar as a *relative* caloric energy unit. All articles of commerce, similar or dissimilar, have relative worth that is woven into the fabric of our behavior."

"OK. A value exists by virtue of it being compared to another item. Assume humans were the sole occupants of the earth and rice was their single source of food. Each human could gather as much rice as they desired from the field. Rice would be valueless."

"True. Value is a creation of the mind."

"Value exists because I think it."

"The price to earnings ratio (P/E) is a common yardstick to measure the value of a bolt. If a company has 100 shares outstanding, and earns $1 for the year with a value of $10, the P/E is ten. Reassess the record for bookkeeping irregularities to ascertain the reliability of the report."

"OK. I will be on the alert for Eddy Roper barking, "Round and round they go, can you find the peanut under the shell"?."

"A crop price reflects contemplated produce discounted for inflation."

"Wait a minute. This sounds like flatulence off the high ground. Contemplated means looking into the future and we may look but we cannot see."

"Correct. When you buy a stake you are saying a novena."

"You pray for nine days?"

"Bulmer, pay heed; a firm can be assessed on the basis of earnings before interest, taxes and amortization (EBITA). Companies that have high debt or capital expense (cable, communications, media and utilities) can be measured by the EBITA."

"Hold the mayonnaise. A business may no earnings and they cook a pot of alphabet soup to underweight their lack of success."

"Yes."

"Buying a ship can be a celestial voyage."

"Dividends are paid to common stockholders out of the firm's profits. They can be a significant part of total receipt for the long-term investor. A dividend-paying ticker will lose less gelt in a deteriorating market then a similar non-dividend-payer because the income will support the resource. A business that consistently pays or furthers its dividend is believed to be secure financially and growing. This firm should command a higher reserve marker than a similar firm with a less favorable payout history."

"What is a value manager?"

"Mapower Kneebone is a value manager. He buys goods that he believes are cheap."

"How does he know it is cheap?"

"The metrics in use by Mapower are: P/E, P/E versus industry, book value, price to book value versus industry, enterprise breakup value, price to sales ratio, price to cash flow per share, and past high/low points. Kneebone will apply an estimate of hoped for earnings. Past P/E will be considered."

"Professor, if a company is at a five year low for its P/E, does he believe this to be a green light? Is it a red light if the multiple is at a five year high?"

"If the P/E it is at a five year high, he will consider the equity to be ritzy, and make the judgment it has limited upside potential. If the ratio is near its five year haunches, he will recap the forces that he believes have shrunk the number."

"Hold the ketchup. How is Kneebone different than Maleva, the gypsy woman on the boardwalk in Atlantic City?"

"Mapower earns $750,000 a year reading reports. She is less skillful than he because she applies her predictive talent to the future. He will study the past and use this information to foretell the morrow."

"Aha. Mapower is uniquely gifted because he can see backwards and forwards, and that is why he drives a new Jaguar convertible while she transports in a bicycle."

"Upon completion of study of what Kneebone considers relevant information, he will purchase a pledge."

"What is a growth manager?"

"Cornelius Card is a growth manager. He looks at the same information as Kneebone but arrives at different conclusions. Cornelius believes the coming proceeds expansion will be the principal driver of the tag price, and he is less concerned about buying the stock inexpensively. He is more likely to purchase a resource that has displayed upward ticker momentum with the hope of continuing gains."

"How does he determine that a marker has peaked?"

"He will await divine inspiration."

"Cornelius and Mapower are overconfident. Both believe they can see the eventual from a different vantage point. Each interprets information that will support their belief."

"Do you know what a belief is?"

Bulmer scratches his head.

"A belief is an idea I hold to be true."

"Beliefs are not true or false. They are not facts or scientifically provable. They are thoughts that you possess that can be changed. What is true cannot be false. What is fact cannot be fiction."

"How do long-term performance results compare between growth and value managers?"

"They approach equality. We have to look at *risk adjusted returns.*

Since the value manager buys cheap inventory, it is assumed he incurs less risk than a growth manager who buys Park Avenue furniture. It is not possible scientifically to measure this because of the subjective nature of equity selection."

"What do you mean?"

"The concepts of a value/growth manager are fictitious. Each one *creates in his mind* the reasons why he should buy. The market sets the worth of a security at a given moment. The toll is absolute reality and cannot be cheap or expensive. If a rag is at a five year high, it does not mean it is forbidden to go higher. If a bolt is in the basement, it does not follow that it must go higher. The basic premise of an investor is that man will progress in providing improved goods and services that will translate into higher harvest scores."

"I will be dead over time, please clarify."

"Man's cadence of progress resembles a coin that has been altered to favor heads 55% of the time. If you flip this coin one thousand times, how many heads would you expect?"

"About 550."

"This leaves 450 tails. Out of 450 tails do you accept that streaks of five, ten, twenty tails can occur?"

"Yes."

"The bias in the coin toss equates to man's pursuit of improvement. If you examine the history of man, the big screen reflects the dramatic enhancements in the quality of goods and services produced. There is no evidence, nor has it been argued, that man has reached the last mile of his conscious ability."

"Eureka. There will be negative sequences of investment results that will be ironed out with salutary time."

"Yes. This does not mean you buy, hold and freeze."

"Explain, please."

"Your investments must be actively monitored. If you accept my strong suggestion to *buy index funds,* you will be incapable of making mistakes."

"There is no sizzle to index funds."

"If a sizzling steak remains on the grill, it will be burnt."

"I am attracted to stocks that are selling at low historical P/E. Is there a study that rates their performance?"

"A research project has shown that using a three year track record and creating one group of equities that performed in the top 10% (winners) and another group in the bottom 10% (losers), the following year the winners will be expected to deliver minus 10% while the losers' will be plus 30%."

Bulmer's four legs are shaking.

"Beelzebub. What do you think?"

"One cannot say the conclusions of one study present truth. Intuitively, if the seed of a muscular company with a positive future is selling at a historical low, I believe there is less risk in owning it compared to a similar stock bought at a historical high."

"The costly security has little escape for error."

"Correct. Depending on market circumstance, it may tumble on untoward news."

"How does one factor in anticipated extension for valuation purposes?"

"The ratio is price/earnings/growth (PEG). If the stock has a P/E of 10 and it is anticipated it will grow at a 20% rate the next five years, it would be believed to be undervalued relative to its presumed growth rate."

"The critical phrase is presumed growth rate."

"Yes. The Smell-Bomber Soap Company makes soap used for personal hygiene. Today it has 50% market share, up from 10% ten years ago. Management has advanced revenue and proceeds consecutively each of the last ten years by product improvement and diversified soap offerings. Smell-Bomber's major competitor has 40% market share, down from 80% ten years ago, and has not changed its product line."

"You are telling me Smell Bomber has been feeding off the flesh of its major competitor who has not moved to stanch the bleeding."

"Yes. The people in the foreign country Hairy Armpit Land are beginning to bathe with soap they received as samples from Smell-Bomber that is the first soap company in the country. The population of Hairy Armpit Land is huge, and although the people prefer natural odors, soap usage is increasing."

"What do smelly people have to do with revenue?"

"Let me continue. The management of Smell-Bomber has been constant the last ten years. Stock options are not used for compensation. The firm maintains a pension but has never used its excess funds to prop-up profits. The outfit is debt free and uses cash flow to fund capital expenses for new products."

"On and on, when do you stop?"

"Details and chance make the pudding of investment. You can eliminate the details if you *buy index funds,* and a helping of the risk."

"No. Please continue."

"Smell Bomber's accounting is ultra-conservative. Revenue is not recorded until cash is received."

"Is there more?"

"Smell Bomber has improved results at a 7% rate each of the last ten years; the management has been successful at capturing market share from its prime competitor; it improves and adds to its product line; soap is a product it's existing customer base will continue to buy; it is the first company to sell in Hairy Armpit Land that is a potentially massive market."

"This is not a fun stock to own."

"One can plan that Smell-Bomber will continue to produce earnings advancing in the neighborhood of 7%. A different company without similar characteristics would not replicate the consistency of Smell-Bomber."

"I observe this refers to price/earnings/growth. Unless earnings exhibit a high degree of reliability, projecting profits is gaseous."

"Yes, able student. The technical school of analysis believes it can look at a chart and predict the movement of the flight. The technician holds to magical points on the chart. A support level is a point from which the bird will not decline unless there is large negative volume, or news. If the stock crashes a support level, the technician creates a new support level. A resistance level is a juncture where a stock has difficulty surpassing. If it crosses the resistance level it is said to have broken away. The technician will create a new resistance level."

"Hold the wire, Meyer. Do technicians get paid for their work?"

"Yes. It is a high-paying profession."

"I believe Maleva is more honorable than a technician."

"Why?"

"When Maleva makes a prediction, she sticks by it and she does not suggest you place your money on her soothsaying. The technician can never be wrong because when his support or resistance level is pierced; he awaits an awakening to declare the amended threshold."

"One should not throw out the learned work of the technician. It offers worthwhile historical data that can be a small part of your decision-making process."

"Does trading volume enter into valuation?"

"An actively traded equity, one that exceeds average daily trading volume of 1,000,000 shares, will have a small spread. The difference between the bid and offered will be pennies. You should be able to trade at a cost close to its last execution. Being able to execute competitively indirectly adds value."

"You mention one has to discount expected earnings for inflation to appraise the current value of a company. How do you do this?"

"Inflation rates rise or fall as a result of: interest rates, productivity, currency valuations, growth/recession, government spending, consumer spending, business spending, politics, demographics and tax policy."

"Whose job is to measure that?"

"Economist. They entertain the same task as Cockermouth. They attempt to get a fix on the future."

"What is their record?"

"Unreliable. Man has endured oracles with the echo of the first spoken word."

"Have the modern prodigies of economics and finance outperformed their earlier brethren? Can they construct a house without ambiguity?"

"No."

"Forecasting inflation is a crapshoot?"

"Yes. There are two other elements to measure expected earnings. The riskiness of the asset compared to what your money would earn on a five-year T-note."

"OK. You showed me the paradigm of consistent earnings in Smell-Bomber Soap Company that would reduce the riskiness of its tag price."

"Smell-Bomber would have less relative risk than other firms but not be risk-free."

"Why?"

"There are three determinants of the merit. If a bear market has swept in lower numbers, many equities will lose value."

"Do you mean in a sinking market Smell-Bomber could capsize despite its excellent history and prognosis?"

"Yes. If the soap industry changes in an injurious fashion, Smell-Bomber will backslide."

"Give me an example, please."

"A water shortage and people wash less by government decree."

"What is the third determinant?"

"Company specific challenges could arise."

"Please, give me examples."

"Smell Bomber could incur extended labor strife causing reduced production and earnings. They could be acquired. Key management may retire, die or leave. The paramount adversary could revive itself through marketing and a new product line to recoup lost revenue. There could be a shortage of ingredients to manufacture soap, causing reduced production. Product liability litigation could injure the firm."

"Smell-Bomber could disappoint."

"Yes. The act of estimating expected income is rife with doubt. Valuation is a moving target demanding the skills of an archer and the smile of the Gods."

16

WHAT LIES BENEATH

"My dear friend Bulmer, what did you filter from our discussion on valuation?"

"The pasture is a bed of mines demanding sure footedness, quickness, and the tap of Gene Kelly. Does the field bear fruit for a successful passage?"

"Yes. The market has doled out fortunes for the well prepared and blessed. How would you find a property that you might invest in?"

"My record is suspect and I need help."

"You want to find value where its perception does not exist."

"Clarify, please."

"If a well-known company has a stud with a history of consistently good performance, and its prospects are constructive in a positive market climate, it is likely the market has noticed value and bid it up."

"What do I look for?"

"You look for a company, small or large, that has not a designer price tag."

"Yes. Our conversations have pointed up the concept of valuation is murky."

"Correct. When you buy, it counts what you pay. If your intent is to cash in, the sum you pay is the basis of your gain/bane."

"Buy low, sell high."

"Do you permit overconfidence to summon the future?"

"No."

"Good. It follows that you accept you will not be able to call market bottoms/tops."

"That's right."

"As of guideline if your trade is within 20% of the top/bottom, you have succeeded. There will be times when you will catch a bottom that will be exhilarating. You will feel brilliant. The reality is you have been lucky. Do not ignore the presence of chance in your investment results. Occasions will arrive where you buy a security and it falls more than 20%. Do not allow this to upset you, recall your reasons for the purchase, and if they remain sturdy, proceed with watchfulness. Fortune/misfortune will visit your household. Accept them as they are. Learn. Move on."

"I will avoid cursing bad luck and will not equate good chance with great skill."

"Excellent. Do you know what cash flow is?"

"Yes, when my wife Cleopatra, empties my pockets."

"Cash flow from operations is the amount of funds collected by the company for the sale of its products/services, less the amount of money paid out to generate the sales."

"How much came in the cash register and how much went out."

"That's right. The financial health of the company is dependent on taking in more cash than paying out.

A firm may turn-on cash flow by selling assets that may not be beneficial long-term. A company could issue stock/debt to raise chicory that would reduce earnings per share or boost interest cost, perhaps harmful to the enterprise."

"Make money from your business not by selling assets or financial welfare."

"The debt structure of the firm should be run through. How does the long-term debt compare with firms within its industry? If the company has a weighty debt-load, will burdensome economic conditions pressure payments? The markets adjust to prevailing conditions. If the ground is compromised, negative news will be highlighted and amplified."

"Explain, please."

"A company may be able to meet its interest payments, but if it is believed difficulties may ensue, the house could be brought down."

"Examples, please."

"Banks prefer to loan money to firms that do not need it. If the bank concludes your company is headed for turbulent water, they may rein in its existing lines of credit or refuse new applications. If suppliers believe they may not get paid, they may curtail shipments, or demand payment in advance."

"Questionable credit can be a creation of the mind. It can be jeopardous when people are jittery about being paid."

"Yes. In the credit arena, assessment can become reality."

"What other items should I know about credit?"

"Check the credit rating of Standard and Poor's."

"What are pro-forma earnings?"

"Companies use these numbers to reflect their results in the most favorable light."

"Do you mean they are withholding information?"

"No. They lubricate the information."

"Show me, please."

"A company incurs a loss from a discontinued operation. They want you to interpret this as we lost money, but we are not going to do it again. We will have better results because we have cut our misdeeds."

"Are they implying they will not have defeats?"

"No. They are saying they want you to have faith, not question them, nor punish the share sum."

"I bet there are people that will see pro-forma earnings as a reason to buy."

"People will be unloading it based on the same report."

"How do I determine the truth about pro-forma earnings?"

"Do not see them as you would like, but *as they are.*"

"What are profit warnings?"

"A company will announce that it expects to earn less money than was anticipated."

"Why does a company do this?"

"The firm believes the paper will be trampled, and they prefer to accept the thrashing sooner than later."

"Amputate the infected section and apply antibiotics. What are the attributes I should look for in a seed I may purchase?"

"Does the firm have a competitive advantage? Why do their customers buy from them? Will they be able to maintain or prolong this competitive advantage? Do they have pricing power?"

"What is pricing power?"

"Is their product/service sold as a commodity on price? Does the company add value to their product/service not replicated by the competition? Can they raise their tariff with adhesiveness?"

"Please, tell me about growth."

"A sticker will not strengthen without earnings improvement. What has been the historical profit progress of the company? What is the estimated net cash betterment the next five years? Where is the expansion to be generated from?"

"Please talk more about competition."

"Is the company the dominant player in its field? Is it continuing to grow? Are their adversaries developing at their expense? How long has the company dominated its industry? Why will this company strengthen faster than its opponents?"

"What is a barrier of entry?"

"How easy is it for a competitor to enter your field? How much effort is required to duplicate your product/service?"

"Can you give me examples of a barrier to entry?"

"No. You have ignored my strong recommendation to be a passive investor in index funds. You have chosen to be an active individual investor of which few have beaten the indexes. You can be successful. You must learn to think independently, and pick up the spade. You will develop gray matter blisters."

"Let's talk about customers."

"Does the company sell to clients that that will repurchase the product?"

"Consumable products must be replaced."

"And."

"A renewable source of income can be cultivated."

"How does branding fit in?"

"Repeated business can promote brand loyalty that will decrease the chances of the client vanishing."

"Good. Tell me what you think of the nature of customer composition."

"Give me a hint."

"Is it better to have several large customers?"

"I do not think so. If you lose a big customer, your sales will flop. Reliance on a small list of clients can be hazardous."

"What is the company's history of product development through introduction of new lines or product enhancements? Has the company demonstrated an ability to upgrade revenue?"

"Let's go back to brand loyalty."

"What makes the brand unique? Can this singularity be perpetuated? How long has the goods been desirous?"

"How can politics affect a company?"

"Does government funding pay for the company's product? Could the political winds alter? Does the company depend on third party payments (insurance)? If the payer changes its policy, will the firm be affected?"

"What about distribution?"

"How does the product reach the final customer? Is a direct one to one or do layers separate the company from the end client?"

"What is capital expense?"

"Does the company require large sums of money to produce its products (the auto industry)? Will operating cash flow pay the bills? If the firm must finance its operation with debt, is the amount reasonable?"

"OK. A firm with petite debt and generous cash flow from operations is desirable."

"What is the financial health of the customers of the firm? Are the customers prospering and will they continue to buy? Are the clients increasing their sales?"

"Inventory?"

"What is the pace of inventory turnover? Has it enlarged or decreased? How does it compare out with the industry? Apply the same questions to accounts receivable."

"Do you believe in cycles, positive and negative?"

"No. I hold that markets respond to physical laws."

"How?"

"A security tag will continue in a direction until a greater force halts it and may cause redirection. A company may be experiencing a barrage of negative forces that drive its number down; until these forces abate the price will seep to its lowest level."

"This is a yellow light. If the asset is flagging, one might wait until the forces settle."

"True. Clear vision does not mean the merchandise will appreciate. The lady of chance makes an appearance. Luck and skill are entwined."

"Let's talk about management."

"Not today. I believe management is the pre-eminent element of a company's success. We will devote tomorrow to management. We will finish up with concepts. Do you know what relative strength is?"

"No."

"Relative-strength measures the performance of the equity applicable to the market. If a ticket has a rating of 90%, it means it has behaved better than 90% of the market."

"I got it. It is best to own armor with high relative-strength."

"Yes. This is a metric not to be used in isolation but as a patch of the terrain. This is a rearward looking indicator, and cannot tell us where the ticker numeral will be."

"What do you think of business momentum?"

"Business momentum occurs when a firm is executing its strategy successfully. Nothing continues in a straight line, and we face the question when does the progress stop? External factors could cause a company to derail. The value of a vibrant company will reflect advances and retreats. If the firm maintains its combative advantage, forward movement will dominate."

"Are you suggesting that I ignore momentum?"

"No. I do not want you to believe that it is a wizardly tool but one of numerous rulers."

"What do you think of the terms emerging-market and first-to-market?"

"They are words to get you excited to buy. Give me that inveterate religion of strong, growing cash flow from operations and trustworthy reporting. It matters not the title of the book, but its merit."

"What about a young company with a new product in a promising market?"

"If you can respect the risk and you liked its prospects, invest."

"Please go deeper into relative-strength."

"It will be beneficial to search for reasons to explain the relative-strength. Why is a company in the top 10%? What distinguishes this company from the rest of the market? If it is in a cyclical industry, what signs or economic data would prompt you to consider selling?"

"Selling would depend on what I paid."

"Selling is activated because you believe the stake will underperform a similar investment the next six to twelve months."

"Please, go back to relative performance."

"Is the outfit subject to buy out? Has a new product contributed to earnings? Has Cockermouth touted the ticker? Did the company restructure? Is there unexpected strong demand for a product? What is the life cycle of this fresh demand? Does the company provide a product that is in short supply? When will the scarcity subside? Has the company repurchased a large amount of its shares? Has the business reported a surprise income broadening? What is the reason for this development, and is it sustainable? Do accounting issues impact the financial reports? Are political forces in play? Have legal changes influenced the outfit? Is the company the subject of takeover rumors? Are demographics a factor? Is there new management?"

"Please give me ideas on how to value a stock."

"How does the net gain of the company compare with its industry? Search for reasons to explain discrepancies."

"Can I rely on Dr. Cockermouth to find a winning equity?"

"Does Augar publish a performance report?"

"No."

"Augar will produce reports that can be of worthwhile assistance in selecting an investment. When he dons his robe, cap and wand to proclaim a marker target, consider this number as reliable as one you would receive from Maleva."

"What about upgrades/downgrades?"

"Augar will cover a basket of produce. His job is to provide ammunition for Gasport Earnshaw (money-maven) to traffic sales. Cockermouth is an artful augur who has a five-tier rating system: strong buy (it will appreciate unless it depreciates and he has received visual and auditory positive information from an unknown source), buy (same as above without visual input), hold (he does not know what to do, and his unknown mentor is mute), sell (negative visual input), strong sell (disturbing visual and auditory impressions from the mysterious agent)."

"What happens when Dr. Cockermouth moves the horse from a hold to a strong buy?"

"The company is large with many Gasports. These infantryman will contact their clients and advise them of Augar's excitement to induce them to buy."

"What happens?"

"The integer will rise with upward volume."

"You deride Dr. Cockermouth because of his suspected hallucinations, but he has the power to create millions of dollars."

"True. clairvoyants can create short-term bonanzas. The market will adjust to the thrust of Augar in a matter of days and set its figure."

"Do you mean Augar will have a short term-effect and the market will decide what it is worth?"

"Yes."

"What happens if Dr. Cockermouth issues a strong sell?"

"It does not happen."

"Why. Does the silent source report sell situations?"

"Maybe, but Augar considers this information unreliable."

"What is money flow?"

"They are transactions that are of 10,000 shares or more. If these trades resulted in a rise in share worth, the money flow is positive."

"What does this tell us?"

"The majority of investments come from mutual funds and retirement plans. When these institutions bid it up, positive force is created. The challenge of momentum is to discern where it stops."

"Please comment on profit warnings."

"Shares are fueled by quarterly earnings reports."

"One minute. We have agreed the reliability and quality of reports can be suspect. Why do they exert such great influence?"

"The historical consciousness of Wall Street is that the premium measure of value is earnings, past and future. Stock soothsayers estimate expected quarterly results. If the company expects they will not meet the analyst number, they will issue a press release deemed a profit warning."

"What happens?"

"The share shape will decrease."

"By what amount?"

"It will depend on the monetary level of the market, the valuations of the company sector, and the expectations of the individual firm."

"In good times it will decline less and bad times it will recede more."

"Yes."

"How useful is price gainers/losers to find a prize?"

"Based on the percentage movement, one may find a worthwhile consideration. Do not believe a large increase/decrease in share value is predictive. You have to review the size of the change relative to near-term and long-term infrastructure."

"What is near-term and long-term?"

"Near-term is less than one year. Long-term is more than three years. Review the questions that you would ask to examine the relative-strength, and apply them where there that has had a large flux in daily share movement."

"What can I learn from peregrines that have an aerial daily trading volume?"

"Large volume, up or down, is a symptom. Why has the volume escalated? Are there reasons rooted in logic, emotion or confusion? Do not admit your emotion to the analysis. Track it for a week, a month, and three months. Has the volume expanded on a consistent basis? Why?"

"I am weary by the dump truck of questions you have unloaded."

"Buy index funds and free up your mind."

"Please finish with moving-average analysis."

"The average daily price of the rag is calculated for 10 days, 21 days, 50 days and 200 days. The results are plotted on a graph to detect trends."

"If the grouse has a downward slope for 200 days, should I avoid it?"

"What are the reasons for the misfortune? What value do you place on the stock at this moment?"

"Do I think the admission is cheap relative to its prospect?"

"Correct."

"One cannot avoid joining the ranks of the soothsayers."

"Yes."

17

CHARACTER

*There is nothing, absolutely nothing
a man cannot forget, except himself,
his own character.*

—Schopenhauer

"Did you sleep well?"

"My sleep was punctuated by at tickertape."

"Do you know what a board of directors is?"

"No."

"It is a group of people who oversee the operations of a company. They should represent the interests of shareholders foremost."

"Are the directors independent?"

"There are directors who served as officers of the firm and independent directors."

"If the chief executive officer (CEO) sits on the board, would there be a conflict of interest?"

"Yes. The board votes on executive compensation and stock options."

"The CEO has voting authority on his pay and benefits? Gee, that's a sweet position to be in."

"Yes. The CEO does not own the company but he may act as an owner to influence his monetary benefits. In good times many boards allow the CEO to fill in the numbers on his paycheck."

"I think an independent board would be better for us."

"The management of a company will have a huge effect on the success. Management behavior is not limited to the operation of the enterprise. Personal, moral and legal issues will stir a stock sum. Equity tickets fluctuate according to the emotional climate. If it is a sunny day and unwholesome news is released about a company officer, the damage will be mitigated. If thunderclouds fill the sky, open your umbrella."

"How does one gauge the effectiveness of management?"

"Look at the history of the performance relative to its peers. Past success does not assure the future but it is a good start. How long has the CEO been at the helm? What was his last position and why did he leave?"

"That is sensible but do I have access to reliable information?"

"No. What is available is superficial gloss. It does not change the vital value of knowing the competence, integrity and character of the CEO."

"How does character to come into play?"

"The CEO operates with intense pressure to produce quarterly profit locomotion at or above expectations. A person's true character is exposed by stress."

"Please, give me an example."

"He might skim off excess pension funds."

"Is that legal?"

"Yes. It does not violate an accounting rule, and it will obscure the operating results for the quarter."

"Can I depend on management?"

"You rely on the trust of management. Many material episodes occur in the life cycle of a company, and one depends on management to enlighten the shareholders."

"You want management to be honest despite what the disclosure of information may have on the sticker price."

"Yes. It would be silly to believe we can entrust blindly on management."

"How do I check?"

"Review prior management communication with the public. Has time tested their truthfulness?"

"Please tell me more about honesty."

The course of true anything never does run smooth. Samuel Butler

"Is this a course in philosophy?"

"Emotion can combat honesty."

"How?"

"A CEO becomes emotionally embroiled with his faltering firm that could cause him to be unaware corporate pestilence."

"Do you mean that could be cracks in the fuselage but the captain will proceed headlong?"

"Yes. I will relate the tale of MegaRon Energy."

"Is this a true soap opera?"

"Yes. Once upon a time, MegaRon Energy was believed to be one of the ten largest companies in the United States with scores of billions of dollars in revenue."

"That explains the mega part."

"MegaRon called itself an energy company with many activities of which they were a world leader in trading energy contracts."

"What does trading energy contracts mean?"

"MegaRon would buy a contract to deliver electricity and sell the contract to another party."

"I sell baseball cards. Same thing."

"One day MegaRon reported a $1.2 billion cataclysm in one-time charges for various businesses with a net charge of $618 million, compared to a gain of $292 million the year earlier. Revenue inflated 49% to $47.6 billion from 30 billion."

"They lost a lot of romaine but they boosted the business a bunch."

"One week later the CEO of MegaRon, Hogg Leech, said ""the company was awash in cash, there would be no more unusual write offs and the investigation by the SEC into the company's trading activities would declare them pure as the Pope."" When pressed to detail how the $1.2 billion loss occurred he replied ""numbers are my weak point."""

"Encore."

"It was known that MegaRon had more than 300 special purpose entities that accounted for 40% of MegaRon's sales."

"What is a special purpose entity?"

"A special purpose entity holds a contract with a firm to provide goods/services or share investment adventure. The transactions between MegaRon and its special purpose entities were not disclosed in MegaRon's financial reports."

"Wow. Do you mean they could project assets and weed out liabilities?"

"Yes. MegaRon reported gains realized with a special purpose entity but omitted charge-backs with the same entity."

"Is that kosher, to count the wins and ignore the mishandling?"

"Several weeks passed, and MegaRon said its debt payments far exceeded its cash. Days passed while MegaRon's demise is being baked. Traders sitting opposite MegaRon on contracts have diarrhea and parched throats. The stresses on MegaRon accumulated."

"Something will give."

"MegaRon is a breath away from having its bench broken."

"Hold it. What does a broken bench have to do with the story?"

"In Italy, a business would keep a bench in front of its store. If it was unable to pay its loan to the bank, the bank would send a man to break the store's bench."

"What about the energy traders?"

"MegaRon Energy was one of the world's largest traders, and it had $18.7 billion in outstanding contracts. These deals would have to be unwound if MegaRon hit an iceberg. There could be billions of dollars in seepage."

"Did MegaRon affect other companies, or markets?"

"The Treasury market experienced rough seas because of perceived strength in the economy driving up rates, and rumors about MegaRon Energy's positions on futures contracts."

"What happened next?"

"The day hastened and MegaRon Energy declared bankruptcy. It tabulated as the biggest bankruptcy immemorial. The court papers stated assets of 49.8 billion with liabilities of 31.2 billion."

"Beelzebub. Their assets surpassed their liabilities by more than $18 billion. Why the bankruptcy?"

"Undisclosed liabilities were buried in their special purpose entities and phantom assets."

"Did there accountants exposed this to the public?"

"No. During the year their accounting firm received $52 million in fees, half for consultation and half for auditing."

"What were the topics of consultation?"

"The creation of special purpose entities."

"What were the special purpose entities to do?"

"They were to pump revenue and income, and secrete liabilities."

"Was this legal?"

"Yes. The accounting rules were not broken."

"Do you mean an accounting firm can defraud investors without fracturing accounting rules?"

"Yes."

"$26 million in consultation fees, hmm, do you think this influenced the audit of the company?"

"A $26 million consultation account provides mountains of escarole. I believe the richness of this contract would effect the auditing of the firm."

"How?"

"The accounting firm would cooperate with the Hogg Leech to present their financial reports in the most favorable light, and withhold information that may be hurtful."

"The accounting firm is under the sheets with the Hogg Leech. This may be XXX rated. I remember fooling around with Mrs. Oxenham when we were teens. My underwear got sticky."

"The next day it was reported in the news five large Japanese money market funds suffered big losses because of holding MegaRon paper."

"That is astounding; money market funds were taken by MegaRon."

"Yes. Moreover, the firms that manage the money market funds were devalued."

"The ripple affect."

"The next day the Big Five accounting firms attempted to allay the concerns of investors regarding financial reports. They said they would cooperate to improve disclosure regarding transactions prominent in the MegaRon bankruptcy. They did not discuss the details of the MegaRon reports that overstated income by $600 million in a four year interval. Mirrors Inc., MegaRon's accounting firm, had admitted that there was improper accounting the prior years, but believed the tens of millions of dollars in question was immaterial."

"Get out. Mirrors Inc. had the audacity to allow the Hogg Leech to puff profits."

"Yes. The investing public was buying shares of MegaRon based on Mirrors Inc. faulty auditing."

"Mirrors Inc. shoveled in $52 million in fees from MegaRon, and whipped up accounts leaving investors with a barf bag."

"Correct. MegaRon declared it made an error by inflating shareholder equity by $1 billion. Mirrors Inc. would not comment about how they missed this error."

"That is not surprising. If Mirrors Inc. did not believe overstating reports by tens of millions of dollars mattered, what is a billion dollars here or there in shareholder equity?"

"Although the overstatement of a billion dollars in shareholder equity did not affect income, it did present a false picture to the bond rating agencies that maintained an investment grade report for MegaRon."

"Why is the credit report pivotal?"

"MegaRon used a mountain of debt to finance their operations, and their trading required the perception that they could meet their obligations. If a firm harbored the smallest doubt that MegaRon could complete an energy contract, it would discontinue operations with MegaRon."

"Next."

"A couple of days later, the largest independent electricity company lost 20% of its value."

"Why?"

"Calclimb, the electric company, was being associated with MegaRon Energy."

"Why?"

"Both companies inhabited the energy sector. The market lambasted a sector when one of its members is cremated. Investors believed that since MegaRon choreographed their financial reports, other energy enterprises could follow this path."

"Was Calclimb run in a similar fashion to MegaRon?"

"No. Calclimb did not engage special purpose entities, nor had their financial reports been materially suspect."

"How were the outfits the same?"

"Both companies traded energy contracts but for different reasons. MegaRon acted as a trading house to make money from the spread between what they paid for a contract and what they sold it for. Calclimb bought contracts for their own use in generating electricity and traded for gain."

"And?"

"Both companies carried a large amount of debt but for different reasons. Calclimb had embarked on a construction campaign to build generating capacity. Plants were being built. They are hard assets. One does not know where the money went for MegaRon, but it did not possess a large amount of hard assets relative to its debt."

"You mean Calclimb owned generating plants that would provide income while MegaRon owned cockypants."

"Yes. At the time that MegaRon's bench was broken, the banana market had been slipping for 18 months. I believe the stock market responds to physical laws, an object in motion will continue in motion until met with a greater or equal force."

"Materiel market malaise will continue until the appropriate quantity and quality of positive occurrences present themselves."

"Correct."

"Please, go back to Calclimb."

"Calclimb was thought to be at peril with the credit rating agencies."

"Why?"

"The recession and other forces reduce the demand for electricity while Calclimb borrowed heavily to produce more of a product that had weak appeal."

"Please move back to the special purpose entities. How were they shrouded from investors?"

"MegaRon used an obscure accounting rule that permitted then to omit a special purpose entity from its financial records. This omission upped MegaRon's yearly fraud by $45 million and erased $711 million in debt."

"What happened to MegaRon?"

"It proceeded through bankruptcy court in an attempt to conserve assets for its creditors. The case has not been settled. It is expected whispers in the wind will remain."

"The ensuing day a credit agency lowered Calclimb's rating to junk."

"Were there other related occurrences?"

"The next week the owner of the largest natural gas pipeline, in addition to being an energy trader, declared it would reduce capital spending by $1 billion, and sell assets to shore up its balance sheet."

"Contagion is spreading."

"Yes. *Perception is reality.*"

"Did the parade continue?"

"The next day, another energy company issued 60 million new shares, reduced expenses, and sold assets."

"Why?"

"The energy industry infection destroyed a great deal of shareholder wealth, and the companies wanted to quell the nervous stomachs of the investors."

"How did the bond market react?"

"Bond quotes of power companies were unplugged. Energy company shareholders rushed the exits because they doubted liquidity would be present amidst lower electricity bills coupled with poor demand."

"Were the consternations of energy company investors rational?"

"The question serves no purpose."

"Why?"

"The seller of Calclimb believes the worth will deflate and the buyer believes the merit will inflate."

"One person's despair is another person's hope, curious circumstance. Can one measure the terror effect on cost?"

"No. If we turn the page of phobia we will find uncertainty on the reverse side."

"Does that mean as incertitude escalates, trepidation follows?"

"No. Phobia is an emotional response to a stimulus. The individual can choose what to fear and the level of fright experienced."

"You make it sound as though I have free will regarding fright."

"True. With the exception of potential physical trauma, you have a personal choice of tribulation. Fears are akin to beliefs; you can believe/fret as you please. There are not required fears/beliefs."

"Can you give me an example how fear/uncertainty drove a number?"

"Flyco is a diversified company in manufacturing/financial services. Dr. Clocker Pugmire became the CEO ten years ago, and grew a $3 billion operation to $38 billion with steady, explosive profit proliferation."

"Jolly good show. How did he do it?"

"He acquired hundreds of companies and restructured them to yield greater earnings. Clocker would not buy a company unless it immediately added to Flyco's net."

"Enough. Please address the topic of the toll."

"On Friday the market value of Flyco was $30 billion. Monday morning brought a news story that Clocker had bought art paintings in New York and illegally avoided paying sales tax. It was expected Pugmire would be indicted. Flyco lost $10 billion of market value that day."

"Why?"

"Flyco's paper had shrunk from $55 to $15 during the six month period before the news story."

"Why?"

"A prime force was the 18 month market fallback. Flyco had undergone repeated SEC investigations into their accounting."

"What did they find?"

"They found no material irregularities."

"Why are investors aquiver about Flyco's accounting?"

"As a result of the many acquisitions their financial reports are complicated. When you buy a company you receive their assets/liabilities. One has to be a sleuth to track these assets/liabilities as they are woven into the big firm."

"People could not understand their reports; the 18 month regression in the marketplace poisoned the waters of consciousness; the fingertips of investors were pan-fried by MegaRon."

"Yes."

"Were there other transports of the sharp decline of Flyco's shares?"

"Five months prior to Clocker being indicted for tax evasion he announced he would chop Flyco into four companies."

"Why? He raised a seed into a harvest."

"Clocker bemoaned Flyco's share sticker of $45 (it was $58 a month earlier) did not reflect the true value of his enterprise. He stated, if he sectioned the company into four units, shareholder value would augment more than 50%."

"How did the market greet Clocker's proposal?"

"In 30 days the integer was $29.50."

"What about the volume?"

"You are a thinking student. The volume popped with the selloff."

"A mammoth volume selloff of a troubled stake in a distressed market should ignite *observation.*"

"Yes. How would you speculate behavioral finance would describe the events?"

"People are not comfortable with change. If a wounded company initiates change in the midst of a disquiet market, the Gods do not favor the odds. Were there other reasons for the breakup?"

"Having four companies would simplify the accounting. Investors would be able to comprehend the financial statements."

"When the shorts active?"

"They had a barbecue. Large amounts had been sold short."

"Can shorts bring down a share virtue?"

"No. The market climate, and other perceived fundamentals would dictate. A big outstanding short position means there are worthy concerns about the outlook of the asset."

"The shorts can provide helpful information about a company."

"Clocker Pugmire is symptomatic of the affliction of the 1990's."

"How?"

"With the rising asset sums many CEOs saw their chance to raid the company treasury. CEOs in impoverished outfits tagged along."

"Was Clocker of this ilk?"

'Pugmire was one of the highest paid CEOs who cashed in hundreds of millions of dollars in options before the share hit the subbasement."

"What did Clocker do for the rag price the last five years?"

"$10,000 invested yielded $13,936."

"That is a 7% happening. An investment grade corporate bond would have approximated that, with a great deal of less risk."

"True."

"Did Clocker misbehave in other ways?"

"Although the state tax evasion trial is unfinished, the prosecution has constructed a prolific case against him."

"This is America. He is innocent until."

"True. His guilt or innocence is immaterial. His indictment flushed $10 billion of value down the commode in one day. It is believed he borrowed Flyco's money to fund his art purchases."

"Golly, is that on the up and up?"

"The company loan program was set up to aid offices to buy company stock not Monet or Renoir."

"I am getting the impression many CEOs considered their firms free ATMs."

"A CEO of an online brokerage firm that was devoid of income from inception was granted a $75 million pay package."

"Did the board of directors vote this?"

"Yes."

"Shareholders have a problem with boards that plunder the vault to enrich the CEO. What happened?"

"Incensed public opinion pressured the board to greatly reduce the CEO's compensation."

"And?"

"Large mutual funds and pension funds declared they would withhold cash from companies that had boards that were extravagant with executive compensation."

"Did you finish with Flyco?"

"No. The investment community was anxious about the wearisome debt assumed by Flyco to finance its prodigious absorption activities."

"What was its long-term debt ratio to equity compared to its competitors?"

"98.55%"

"I don't understand. They had less debt than other diversified manufacturers."

"Yes. Flyco had been dressed in rags and been burdened by the decomposed paper values of the market pullback."

"What was its P/E versus the industry?"

"36.89%"

"Godfrey Daniel. People thought Flyco was worth about two-thirds less than a similar company. What business was it in?"

"It makes electrical and electronic components, circuit boards, specialty valves, disposable medical products and other specialty products. It manufactures, installs, and operates undersea cable lines and fire and burglar alarm systems."

"I believe those are capital businesses, especially the medical products and fire and burglary alarm companies. Why was Flyco selling at a vast discount to its foes?"

"One can argue although the market dictates the merit that is real, how much is it phobia driven? Is the angst rational? What is the probability that the anxiety laden event will occur?"

"Hey. You are sitting in the tent of the oracle."

"Yes. If we buy Flyco we see a verdant vista, if we sell it we envision a road of dry, yellow-brown weeds.

"How are you different than Augar Cockermouth?"

"We are the same in our quest to sight the impenetrable future. I attempt to lead you to apply unimpaired reasoning to investing. I am not responsible to provide the sales department, neither with motivating ideas, nor to beautify a client that investment banking is hawking."

"You provide the instruments for me assay the land."

"Yes."

"Please revert to Flyco. What was the 52 week high/low?"

"$60.09/$8.25"

"Did business deterioration or a substantial decrease in cash flow explain the downdraft?"

"No. Earnings estimates have been taking down, but not sufficiently to explain the pointed decline in the sticker. If Flyco sold its business units they would fetch more than the current $13.40 per share."

"Why?"

"The market rest in melancholy. Add the floundering, listing management of Flyco, and you get an estimate below enterprise value."

"Is Flyco a buy?"

"Is your stomach reinforced with titanium?"

"Why?"

"Yes, Flyco has hearty businesses with good results and positive cash flow, but it wears an albatross of debt that has been downgraded to junk. If Flyco encounters a liquidity crisis it may find itself at the threshold of default."

"What would cause Flyco to be unable to satisfy its loans?"

"A severe downturn in its businesses that causes the cash flow to turn negative."

"What else could injure Flyco's karma?"

"Its credit rating has been crushed to compost. Their borrowing cost have escalated about 15%."

"Heightened borrowing cost reduces earnings."

"Touché. You are grasping the effects of economic linkage."

"Please tell me about Merry Lynch."

"Elliott Spunky, the New York State Attorney Five Star, administered 100,000,000 lashes."

"Spell it, please."

"Spunky investigated the relationship between the Merry analysts and it's investment bankers."

"What did he find?"

"Analysts were extolling equities their investment bankers were promoting."

"How did Spunky discover this?"

"He uncovered e-mail between prophets and bankers. The analysts commented a few of the issues supported by the bankers were more suitable as fertilizer."

"How did the analysts respond?"

"They put the turd on their recommended list and pick up their pompoms."

"How is an analyst paid?"

"Research is expensive. Cockermouth earns $15 million a year. Merry Lynch does not charge for Augar's sightings or archery. Luton's banking division is the most profitable part of the firm, and their mammoth fees absorb the cost of Cockermouth"

"Other than the lashes, what did Spunky do to Merry?"

"Merry Lynch agreed to remove Luton's control of the analyst, and to make analysts' compensation independent of O'Greedy's department."

"What effect did Merry's deal with Spunky have on the market?"

"Another log on the fire of dissolution."

"Please spare the symbolism."

"The market had been in withdrawal for more than two years."

"I believe independent directors should replace directors who are officers."

"CEO's compensation should be tied to long-term performance and be reflective of industry norms."

"The moral integrity of key officers of the firm should be a prime qualification."

"If the character of the officers is marketable, the shareholders will foot the bill."

"Does the company behave honestly with its employees, customers, investors?"

"Off balance sheet items, special purpose entities, demand expert scrutiny."

"Observe how a major economic event (MegaRon) can influence an economy and a sector."

"Do you mean the cuffing of energy aviators with trading activities?"

"Yes."

"The sprouting of negativism in the economy?"

"Yes. Do not believe accountants protect investors."

"Heed the clout credit rating agencies wield."

"You must cut the line connecting trepidation and behavior."

"What do you mean?"

"If you permit fear to be an element of the decision process, your returns will paint red."

"If I am afraid I will lose money on an investment, I should not sell it?"

"Maybe you should sell; choices are best based on how you expect the stow to perform, on a risk adjusted basis, compared to the performance of where you would put the proceeds of the sale."

"Do you mean I should consider the money a ticket represents as an energy unit, and my job is to use this energy in the best fashion?"

"Yes"

"Can foreboding be a symptom?"

"One has to separate incubus from the happening and apply thoughtful *observation*. It is human and healthy to be afraid. The task is to address the derivative of your apprehension."

"If fear is a stimulus, prices can move violently, and the investor should strip away the fear and *observe.*"

"Yes. In a diseased market climate simple is better than complicated."

"Agreed, if people labor to understand the company, they will look askance. Do companies have character?"

"Yes. It is composed of their history of management culture."

"Are you suggesting companies have personality?"

"Yes. The independent stewardship of the board of directors in cooperation with an effective management of high quality character prepares the field for the produce."

18

REASONS NOT TO BUY

"Today we discuss why not to buy.

Make a list of as many items that would cause you not to buy."

"You want me to be aware of the insecurity of investing?"

"Yes. And it would help you to develop a critical eye how you deploy your energy units."

Got it, next."

"Alongside each reason you would not buy, fill in a reason to buy."

"Yes, if the reason to buy is stronger, the deal may be desirable."

"Yes."

"What about textiles that weave an intriguing yarn?"

"Do you mean firms that have a marvelous technology that will alter consumer behavior?"

"Yes"

"Does the company have earnings?"

"No, or a paucity."

"You are betting on a company that you are not qualified to assess. Few of these firms will pay you back to compensate for the high risk and drain of money."

"I have looked into a company that has a unique medical product that is patented and ready to roll."

"Have you measured the market for its product?"

"No."

"It may be a wonderful product but unless there is a substantial and growing demand, the company may expire."

"My friend loves Mrs. Broadbottoms Cheesecake, should I buy it?"

"It is OK to investigate and decide based on your findings."

"I did a preliminary check on a restaurant and I think I am ready to buy."

"If you complete the research and it indicates a buy, do it. If you do not desire to maintain an ongoing study of the company, do not buy it."

"How much weight do you place on cash flow from operations?"

"Observe the last 12 quarters. If you do not find acceptable forging ahead, this may be a reason not to buy."

"What about firms that have recently merged or executed a large acquisition?"

"Wait. Watch the integration. Is the firm realizing the benefits that prompted the change?"

"What do you think about a rag that is selling at a premium valuation?"

"It is OK to buy a ticker with an haute couture tag if you believe it warrants its richness, but limit it to a small segment of your investments."

"My uncle, Spalding Muxworthy, is a physician and he tells me of a new company that will be introducing a product that will cure loneliness. He says I should buy now."

"If you go to the racetrack you will find people who, for a fee, will give you the winner of the next race."

19

WHEN TO SELL

"We enter the booby trapped terrain where peril sits and waits. When does one sell?"

"What are the snares?"

"*You* are the obstacle."

"Aha. The emotional debris one meets with the act of selling. The dreaded ruin served with the wounds of regret."

"Yes. Have you thought about why you would sell?"

"No. But I would begin with the reasons I bought."

"Outstanding. You buy a stock and it moves from \$15 to \$30 in three months."

"Super. That's an annualized bounty of 400%. It might be a good time to take spoils and wait for it to fallback to buy."

"Is your goal to be a short-term trader?"

"No."

"Do you have an enterprise you have been following that you want to buy with the proceeds of the sale?"

"No"

"Has the company disappointed with a quarterly earnings report?"

"No. Let's assume it did."

"What is the reason for the reduced net? Is it a company/industry issue? Can management right the ship? Has the firm has faced a similar problem? How have they responded?"

"What about analysts forecast?"

"It is OK to look. They may change their numbers slowly, and their first revision may not depart a great deal from the first forecast."

"You mean Dr. Cockermouth may not address his error and will anchor close to his initial number?"

"Has the company changed its capital structure?"

"How?"

"Is there a large amount of new debt, or a torrent of new shares?"

"Why does debt concern you?"

"Debt can be good or bad depending on how the funds are used, and the market's perception of the company's ability to repay."

"I would look at its competitive industry position."

"Good. What would you look for?"

"Has an adversary supplanted one of the firm's products?"

"Has the outfit shifted into an area you fail to understand, or do not believe favorable?"

"What about the dividend?"

"If is being reduced or eliminated, is it because of a lack of funds, or better use in the business?"

"You believe in setting price targets?"

"I have not broken bread with Augar Cockermouth."

"Why?"

"I believe you ride a winner until circumspection advises you to dismount."

"Do you mean, if I buy at $10 and it reaches $40 within five years, I should not sell?"

"The number $40 and five years originated in your mind, and did not affect the stub behavior. When you own a stake you are placing a wager on its fate. The booty you have in a position is independent of the future value."

"Are you suggesting I should abrade the past and view the investment as though I was buying it today?"

"Yes. If you sell to reap riches, you are selling because of apprehension of loss."

"Is not fear healthy?"

"Yes. It can be but not when fright is based on fear."

"What about an unproven performer that scoots 700% within one year?"

"A biotech outfit?"

"Yes."

"The biotech industry owns a vault full of the best classical stories."

"Curing/mitigating disease and improving the quantity/quality of life."

"Yes. It is populated with our best scientists and wears the label of a hyper-competitive industry."

"What does that have to do with if I should rake in a bounty?"

"Nothing. Does the company have revenue/profit?"

"No. It has promise."

"The market will pay for promised to limit. An outfit without revenue or other measurable prospects will be a grand slam or a strike-out."

"What are other measurable prospects?"

"The firm could have drugs in late third stage trials for the FDA."

"What does that mean?"

"The drugs are close to approval for manufacturing."

"Cash is coming."

"Maybe, one has to consider the efficacy of the drug, size of market, competition and marketing ability."

"Should I sell?"

"If you are a riverboat gambler, hold on, you may be dealt a slew of winning hands. You may want to chance a part of your winnings by placing a stop order."

"What is a stop order?"

"The tag is $70, you place a stop order at $60, and if it hits or passes $60 your order becomes a market order, and is executed at the next offering.

"My sale could be higher or lower than $60?"

"Yes. This can be a great danger in a volatile market."

"How?"

"You have a stop order at $60. It closes at $61. The company reports a colossal, unexpected detriment in the morning, and a stadium of investors hit the sell button. Buyers are hidden in the catacombs. The seed opened at $35. It has pierced your $60 threshold and your order is done at $35."

"Mother of Grace my iceberg is rotten. Can this be avoided?"

"Place a stop/limit order at $60."

"Please define."

"If the ticker hits $60 or less it becomes a limit order at $60 that means your order will be filled at $60 or better."

"I like that."

"The same events played out as above, and your order is unfilled because it opened at $35 (it pierced the $60 stop part) but did not rise to $60. You are holding a claim that has lost 42% of its energy overnight."

"Are you suggesting I am better off selling out at $35 despite believing I could sell it at $60?"

"No. How would you compare this asset with a similar one?"

"I lost a wheelbarrow of money, my pupils are red, and you want me to partake in comparative analysis."

"Yes. Gains/losses do not exist on open positions."

"Are you asking if it is a buy/hold/sell at $35?"

"Yes."

"And you want me to emotionally accept the $35, and wash away the memories of $60."

"Yes."

"Please explain why I should hold a position as opposed to buy/sell."

"One should hold because the reasons you bought it had not changed markedly."

"Dr. Cockermouth rates a tag hold because he expects it to perform as the market does."

"It is senseless to own an article you believe will copy the market."

"Why?"

"You can arrive at market performance while reducing risk by buying an index fund."

"People believe when I sell, other than using the proceeds to fund retirement or improve the quality of life, I am admitting my rationale for buying was marred."

"No. To assume you can envision what is to be is troublesome."

"Hence, that creates the need to affix attention."

"Yes."

"What about a ticket that has been a huge provider becoming 40 to 50% of your portfolio. Is it time to lighten up?"

"Do you believe the accumulation poses too great a risk?"

"I would look at the core nature of the business and estimate its immediate and longer-term prospects. The results would lend a handle on the relative risk."

"If the game conditions are favorable keep your winners in motion, and use stop orders as circuit breakers, if you are cream pied."

"Are there other reasons not to sell?"

"We are going to develop sell strategies."

"Good."

"As you encounter retirement it will be a good time to sell part of your shares and use the proceeds to buy fixed income securities."

"That will reduce risk."

"Yes. When you are enamored with a company and your genius in picking it, sell."

"Why?"

"This generally occurs in expensive markets."

"I will net a good sum."

"Yes. If the product your company produces becomes subject to severe price competition, sell."

"Profits will be pinched."

"Yes. Unload when competitors report negative news other than management problems."

"Bad sector news can drag down members of that club."

"Yes. You may want to repurchase at a lower cost. Consider selling when harmful information comes out."

"Why?"

"It may be the start of a series of pernicious news, notably during bear markets."

"Should I consider a capital gains tax when selling?"

"No. The decision to sell is based on objective criteria. Smile if you have been blessed."

"How much time should I devote to selling?"

"Develop the habit of inspection to find produce to sell."

"This will change my mind set of buy/hold."

"Yes."

"Do I consider commissions in selling?"

"No. Transaction costs are part of investing and should not influence decisions."

"What if the pony runs up quickly and dramatically?"

"Sell, if the hype is believed to be artificial and temporary. Buy back at a better figure."

"What about a dividend paying vendible that cuts its payout?"

"This could be an early warning. Sell, and replace with a firm that has fertile dividends."

"What about a sticker that has been boosted by a brokerage report?"

"Sell. In a couple of days the price may fall back and you can repurchase."

'What about when exceptionally good news sparks movement?"

"Consider selling between 11 and noon during the peak frenzy."

20

CHOOSE

"Good morn Bulmer, welcome to the laboratory of picking an investment."

"Is this a live experiment?"

"Yes. We will explore the numbers and outlook of Citicorp and Bank of America."

"Good."

"Bank of America it is a giant regional bank. Citicorp is an international Goliath. The following represents the most recent annual report: Bank of America had $38 billion total revenue, 70% was derived from loans and leases with the majority in residential mortgages. Citicorp had revenue of $67 billion, 50% was global consumer and 50% was global corporate (including a major stock brokerage firm).

The first distinction is global versus regional."

"Other differences?"

"Citicorp has balance between consumer and corporate businesses while Bank of America is overweight in residential mortgages Net proceeds for BankAmerica is 17.7%, and Citicorp is 21.5%, 21% better for Citicorp. Bank of America is the biggest bank in California."

"California is the richest state, what happens if the state goes bad?"

"Citicorp is in more than a hundred countries."

"Being in many different markets could produce a greater consistency of earnings."

"Bank of America has not made major acquisitions."

"They look for internal headway."

"Yes. Citicorp bought a bank in California that that will add 355 branches moving them up 12 to 4 in size. Citicorp acquired the second largest bank in Mexico."

"Why?"

"Mexicans are the fastest widening demographic in the United States, and Mexico is the second biggest trading partner with the United States."

"When the U.S. economy does well, it will flow to Mexico."

"Citicorp bought a large leasing firm."

"They rose by acquisition. How do they manage the new arrivals?"

"Citicorp has been able to reduce expenses at least 15% on purchased companies."

"What is their plan to enhance revenues/remunerations of the newcomers?"

"Citicorp excels at cross-selling their services. Their typical branch averages 3.5 products per household. They propelled revenue 20% quarter over quarter on a small regional bank they bought last year."

"Who is the biggest player in credit cards?"

"Citicorp, they hold a balance of $109 billion."

"What about the foreign loan loss exposure for each company?"

"With extensive overseas operations, Citicorp faces abundant exposure. This leads to a diversified earnings or debit stream."

"How do the companies match up on loan loss provisions?"

"Estimating loss reserves is art and chance, and based on the good faith and skill of management in measuring the credit quality of its loan book."

"Risk exists for under or overestimation of loss reserves."

"Bank of America had 11.1% of revenues in loss reserves; Citicorp had 10.2%. These are estimates, and the conservative management of Bank of America would over-reserve."

"Do you have a number on Citicorp's expense reduction for the year?'

"$1 billion as they reconstitute their global technology with their gatherings; they expect to realize uncollected earnings from the leasing company they bought."

"What are the dividends?"

"Bank of America has an attractive 3.7%; Citicorp is 1.8%."

"That's a big divide. Why?"

"Citicorp's forward strategy is to expand worldwide by buying companies that can maximize opportunities."

"They cannot execute an aggressive marching plan without cash. Has Bank of America been increasing its dividend?"

"Yes. 10% for each of the last five years."

"Citicorp is not competitive on dividend. What about bestow behavior?"

"$10,000 put in Bank of America five years ago is $12,380? In Citicorp it is $22,548."

"Citicorp paid handsomely to compensate for the less than $1,000 in additional dividends paid to the Bank of America shareholders."

"Interest rates are near historical lows. What occurs when rates rise?"

"It would depend on the state of the economy."

"What you mean?"

"Low interest rates imply a sluggish economy indicating weak demand from the corporate sector. Although credit is inexpensive, companies are not applying because they lack confidence to successfully use their resources. Rising interest rates will amplify the cost of borrowing to the lenders, but they may be able offset this with higher loan demand. Debt is an anathema in today's market."

"Why?"

"More than two trillion dollars in stock value has gone to Valhalla in the last year. Investors eat Rolaids instead of Chuckles. Firms with cumbrous debt loads are viewed as dying elephants seeking their resting grounds."

"Which company do you think would carry more debt?"

"Citicorp has 81.8% debt to capital versus 76.4%."

"Why?"

"Global expansion and the accumulation of companies built debt. Citicorp has rewarded the shareholders with superior renderings achieved on a higher risk adjusted basis."

"What do you think of Citicorp's credit card exposure?"

"How are the delinquency rates?"

"Management believes the worst is behind them, and expects less credit card charge-offs the next six months. This does not mean the exposure to loss has been reduced."

"What is Citicorp's prominent credit cards risk?"

"A worldwide recession visits. People are unemployed and businesses quicksand. Credit card balances go unanswered."

"Are there other items of note?"

"Bank of America is the largest U.S. bank, and expects to make headway with further meaningful cost reduction. Citicorp has a strong balance sheet; it boosted the loan loss reserves by 400 million to $10.5 billion. It has doubled deposits to $142 billion, providing a thrifty source to borrow. Its credit rating was hoisted last year."

"What else?"

"Citicorp has written off two-thirds of its Argentine disaster and three-quarters of its MegaRon boondoggle. It continues its consistent repurchase of shares. Corporate loan failures have leveled off."

"Who has the strongest balance sheet?"

"Bank of America."

"Is it because they have less debt?"

"Yes."

"What was the yearly average net change in total cash flow the last five years?"

"Bank of America was minus $346 million, Citicorp plus 1 billion 638 million."

"How many shares do the companies have outstanding?"

"1.5 billion for Bank of America and 5.1 billion for Citicorp."

"More than triple. Why?"

"Corporations issued currency in the form of shares."

"Citicorp issued shares to buy companies."

"Bull's eye."

"What are the P/Es?"

"P/Es change moment to moment with the asset worth. In the last month Citicorp has lost about 20% of its value while Bank of America is unchanged. Today the trailing 12 month P/E of Bank of America is 15.9, Citicorp is 13.3."

"Why has Bank of America held its value?"

"The market has been stressed the last month. The Bank of America dividend is double that of a money-market account and that will support a ticker during a retrenchment."

"Citicorp is more volatile than Bank of America?"

"Yes. Citicorp's performance has been better than Bank of America's. The five-year earnings per share for Bank of America were 4.4%, Citicorp 14.1%."

"That fits. A company with a high energy rate will be more volatile. Why?"

"Anticipation, Citicorp is expected to outperform its challengers. Weakness in the company/industry/economy will transit the price more than Bank of America."

"What is return on assets?"

"It measures the effective employment of assets."

"How does Bank of America and Citicorp stack up for the last five years?"

'Bank of America was 1.1%, Citicorp 1.4%."

"Citicorp makes superior use of their assets."

"Quite."

"Which do I buy?"

"Are you comfortable with the greater risk and volatility of Citicorp?"

"No."

"Are you willing to trade the enhanced potential reward of Citicorp for the greater stability of Bank of America?"[7]

"Yes. Hmm. One minute please."

21

INITIATION

Daybreak witnesses Socrates, Mogford and Bulmer aboard a 33' sloop in the Aegean Sea. Socrates pilots the wheel. Mogford is at the stern and Bulmer is releasing the spinnaker.

"My students, join me at the fore."

Mogford and Bulmer lumber forward heaving the ship. Socrates ties the wheel and faces them. The wind whipped, bow bent and sea swelled. Bulmer stood, eyes smoky and lit red.

"I am ready to conquer, I am the captain, and I will pick stocks."

The flag on the mast went limp and swells settled. Mogford's ears slackened, eyes heavy and supine jaw.

"I will humbly buy index funds."

Author's biography

Michael Buttacavoli was a financial adviser for a big brokerage securities firm. He worked for the New York Stock Exchange in the Floor Department that reviewed trading operations. In 1971 he started a successful insurance agency in New York City placing fire and liability coverage for businesses. He is a winning poker player who has applied these skills to successful investing. He earned a BA from Brooklyn College majoring in Psychology in 1969.

Buy this book if you are a first-time investor or:

- You are afraid to lose money in the market.

- You believe you can pick financial winners better than everyman.

- You make investment decisions when you are emotionally upset.

- You have difficulty selling stocks that are losers.

- You sold stocks that had gains and failed to sell stocks that had losses.

- You own mutual funds or have a brokerage account.

Tagline: Ignite Behavioral Finance to Bring-In the Money

Reference Notes

TWELVE   PHOTONS

1. Mark Hulbert, "Why Last Year's Winners Falter. A Behavioral Explanation." American Association of Individual Investors Journal 1999, Vol. XXI. No.10.

2. R. Douglas Van Eaton, "The Psychology Behind Common Investor Mistakes", American Association of Individual Investors Journal April 2000, Vol. XXIII, No. 3.

3. James B. Cloonan,"Why Investors Tend to Trade Too Much-And What to Do About It." American Association of Individual Investors Journal July 1997, Vol. XIX, No. 6.

4. Frank Campanale and Brett Shakun, "Behavioral Idiosyncrasies and How They May Effect Investment Decisions." American Association of Individual Investors Journal October 1997, Vol. XIX, No. 9.

5. "Volume, Volatility, Price and Profit. When All Traders Are Above Average." Journal of Finance, Vol. LIII No. 6, December 1998, 1887–1934.

6. "Boys Will Be Boys: Gender, Overconfidence, and Common Stock Investment", Terrence Odean and Brad Barber, Quarterly Journal of Economics, February 2001, Vol. 116, No. I, 261–292.

7. wsj.com

Glossary

advance/decline line   The number of stocks that had increased in price verses the number that have decreased. A broad-based indicator of the breath of the market.

American Association of Individual Investors   A nonprofit organization dedicated to the education of the individual investor. It provides a wide range of helpful, unbiased information. Members meet at local chapters on a regular basis. www.aaii.com Phone: 800 428 2244

annuitize   To receive payments from an annuity.

Annuity   It is a contract offered by a life insurance company. The customer transfers funds to the company with the agreement to receive payments for a specified period. Useful as a supplement to retirement with the benefit of the investment income growing tax deferred. It can be purchased directly from an insurance carrier or a life insurance agent. If you buy from an agent, does the service justify the commission?

asked price   The lowest price a security is offered for sale.

back-end load   A deferred sales charge is associated with B shares of mutual funds. A six to seven year period must expire before the investor is not liable for the deferred sales charge. If one sells prematurely, the sales charge will be deducted from the proceeds. Back-end loads can apply to other types of investments and the details should be reviewed attentively.

balanced fund   A mutual fund holding: common stocks, preferred stocks, and bonds. The purpose is to provide growth in common stock values with income from preferred shares and bonds.

balanced investment strategy   An investment approach of owning stocks and bonds while shunning excessive risk.

barrier to entry   Obstacles posed to an entity that wishes to enter a business. If one wanted to produce automobiles, it would require a large amount of capital.

basis point   One hundredth of a percentage point (0.01), used to measure changes in fixed income products.

bear market   Declining values in securities over a period of time.

Behavioral Finance   A field in psychology that addresses the behavioral aspects of investor decisions. It studies the how and why of the investment process in buying or selling securities. The emotional aspects of investing are highlighted.

below par   A security that is valued at less than face value. If a bond has a face value of $1,000.00 and is being offered for $900.00, the offering is below par.

benchmark   A reference, used for comparison. It is wise for the investor to develop the habit of comparing results with an appropriate benchmark on a regular basis.

Beta   It is a relative measurement to a benchmark. If a bank stock has a beta of 1.00, it has moved in line with other bank stocks. If the beta is 1.10, the stock has moved 10% more than similar bank stocks. Be alert that comparisons are to stocks of a similar nature.

bid price   The lowest price presented to buy a security.

blend fund   A mutual fund that invests in stocks, bonds and money-markets.

blue chip   A big, national company with a history of steady earnings progression with excellent products and strong management.

board of directors   People elected by shareholders to review and guide the business activities of the corporation. If company officers sit on the board objectivity may be compromised. It is desirable for directors to be independent.

bond fund   A mutual fund that invests in bonds. Funds are available to meet various needs: short-term, intermediate-term long-term, treasury securities, mortgage-backed securities, corporate, municipal, high-yield, foreign and emerging market. Compare the expense ratio and credit quality of similar bond funds.

book-entry security   The transaction is recorded electronically without a physical document.

broker-dealer   A firm but that buys and sells securities and executes trades.

bull market   An interval of rising security values.

buy and hold   Buy and hold a stock for a period greater than two years with the expectation you will earn a reasonable profit. It is defunct theory because of the speed of change in today's economy and the rapid movement of markets.

buying on margin   Buying securities on credit by paying for a part of the transaction in cash and borrowing the balance from the broker. If the security declines in value, the broker may make a margin call, requiring you to post additional funds. You will pay an interest rate on the borrowed funds. Consider the lowest margin rate by comparing competing brokers. The use of margin magnifies your results with greater recompense in an up-market and larger losses in a down-market. Volatile stocks purchased on margin can generate a quick margin call if the market goes against the investor. Buying on margin is recommended for experienced practitioners, not beginners.

buy-side analyst   A person who works for an investment company who researches securities for purchase.

callable   A security that can be redeemed by the issuer before the maturity date. If you buy a callable security, are you receiving a call premium? Compare the callable bond with a non-callable bond by interest rates and credit quality.

capital efficiency   The ratio of production divided by cost. The larger the number, the greater the efficiency attained. The concept of producing more product with less resources.

capital flight   Money that abandons an investment. Why is the money leaving? Do you agree with the reason? Is this an opportunity?

capital gain   Profit received from an investment.

capital distribution   Money declared by a mutual fund earned through the sale of securities.

capital intensive   An activity that requires a large amount of money to complete. To start a pharmaceutical company would be capital intensive and financing would be integral.

capital structure   The underpinning, long standing financing of a company that would include long-term debt, common and preferred stock and retained earnings.

cash cow   A company that generates a large amount of cash. How is the cash being used?

cash flow   Cash received minus cash paid out over a segment of time. Is the cash flow increasing? A preferable harbinger to net profit since it is less susceptible to deceit.

cash surrender value   Money received after canceling a life or annuity policy. Before canceling a policy, request a written statement of the costs involved in cancellation and the proceeds.

CD   A Certificate of Deposit is a fixed income product that pays a specified interest for a stated period of time. Payment of principal and interest is a guaranteed up to $100,000. Compare rates with money-markets and municipal money-markets.

Class A shares   Mutual fund shares which carry an up-front sales charge ranging from 4 to 6% of the amount invested. Do not buy unless you intend to hold this fund more than five years.

Class B shares   Mutual fund shares which carry a deferred sales charge between 4 and 6% of the sum invested. These funds tend to have the highest expense ratio. Reject unless you plan to keep this fund more than six years.

Class C shares   Mutual fund shares that carry a sales charge of one percent of the net asset value of the fund each year. These shares afford flexibility making it less expensive to change funds without incurring large sales charges.

closed-end fund   The investment company offers a fixed a number of shares to the public. The shares trade as common stock on an exchange with their value subject to market forces. Open-end fund value is determined by the sum of its holdings.

compounding   The process where an investment multiplies when left undisturbed. If one begets 5% annually, the interest will exceed 5% the second year because one is receiving interest on interest.

consumer confidence index   A gauge on consumer conjecture regarding existing economic situations. A monthly household survey is conducted sampling 5,000 households. The index measures consumer outlook on current conditions (40%) and future expectations (60%).

consumer price index   A monthly guide to inflation that monitors the change in the cost of a group of goods and services such as housing, food, utilities and transportation.

convertible bond   A corporate bond that can be exchanged for preferred or common shares. If the common shares rise in value, one may convert and realize capital appreciation.

convertible preferred   Shares that can be converted to common shares with similar benefits as convertible bonds. You should receive a higher interest rate than a similar convertible bond because the bond is paid first.

cooking the books   Reporting financial results that project an untruthful or misleading picture.

corporate bond   A debt instrument where a firm borrows money, pays interest and repays the sum borrowed at an agreed date. Compare (like quality) corporate bond rates with treasury rates and mortgage-backed securities.

coupon yield   The interest rate stated on a bond.

credit rating   A report by a private independent company. It measures the ability of a company to meet its financial obligations. Observe changes, especially reductions. Appraise the changes effect on the short and long-term performance of the stock.

curbs in   It is a procedure by a stock exchange to mitigate severe price movements that are up or down. Restrictions can be placed on program trading where sell programs are computer generated based on price movement.

current yield   The interest earned for a given duration on a fixed income instrument. The interest changes with the value of the security.

CUSIP   Committee on Uniform Securities Identificaton Procedures. A nine digit number assigned to tradable securities.

debenture   Unsecured debt supported by the financial strength of the borrower not by collateral.

diluted earnings per share   All items that may affect earnings are thrown into the pot: common stock, preferred shares, unexercised options, unexercised warrants and partial convertible debt. By considering all liabilities to earnings, an accurate picture emerges.

derivative security   A security(option) whose characteristics and value depend on an underlying security.

discounted cash flow analysis   An approach to value an investment based on prospective cash flows considering inflation and the time value of money.

dividend   A payment authorized by the board of directors in cash but can be stock. It is paid quarterly from current earnings. Small, young or high octane companies do not pay dividends because they believe the funds can be best used by the company in promoting capital enrichment.

dividend reinvestment plan   Dividends are used to buy additional shares. If you want to add to your holdings of this company, this is a sensible and easy approach.

dollar cost averaging   Investing a stated amount, monthly, regardless of up or down markets. It is a steadfast approach to long-term investing removing the guess work of when to buy.

downgrade   An analyst issues an opinion that the subsequent performance of a stock is negative. If the analyst is influential, the stock will decline in price. If you disagree, a buying opportunity has been created. If you agree, consider waiting several days before selling if the market is balmy. If you hold the stock, be forewarned and apply a critical eye.

downside risk   Estimated loss of value of a security from company, industry, or mart reversals. Your judgment will be subjective and speculative.

earnings surprise   Analyst make earnings predictions for companies. Companies report their earnings on a quarterly basis. If a company reports greater than expected earnings, the stock price will rise (excepting negative news). The tag is bid up because people expect accelerated profit futherance. An injurious earnings surprise will cause a decrease in share value.

economic indicator   Statistical information pointing to trends in the economy. Lagging indicators (unemployment rate) give a picture of the past and predictive indicators (building permits) stare into the future.

ex-dividend   A security that is without the right to collect the announced dividend. The security trades ex-dividend two business days before the date the dividend is paid. The loss of the dividend is reflected in a lowered stake price while trading ex-dividend.

expense ratio   The operating cost of a mutual fund expressed as a percentage of net asset value. It does not include transaction costs that are burdensome, if the fund actively trades. In selecting a mutual fund, the expense ratio should be placed under a microscope and compared with other mutual fund expense ratios. Investment expense has a crucial impact on performance and should be minimized without sacrificing performance.

flexible spending account   A plan offered by an employer where pretax dollars are deducted from the paycheck to fund payment for uncovered medical expense (deductibles or uninsured items). The employee should create a list of expenses eligible under the flexible spending account and have this sum deducted from the paycheck. The deduction is pretax, you are lowering the cost of your noncovered medical expense. Be meticulous in budgeting this expense because unused money will be confiscated.

flight to quality   In times of financial turmoil, people will buy low-risk investments (Treasury Securities).

free cash flow   Operating cash flow (net income+amortization and depreciation) minus capital expenditures and dividends. It is the amount of money remaining after all expenses have been paid including investments. It is unrivalled indicator of current financial health.

front-end load   Sales charges paid for investment at the inception. Are you receiving fair value for the fee you are being charged? Can *you* make the investment and eliminate the sales charge?

full commission   Maximum commission chargeable by a broker for a transaction. Brokers will discount sales charges. Did you ask for a discount? Did you ask if the trade could be done at the minimum commission?

G-7   The group of the seven largest industrial nations created to discuss common economic interests (United States, Japan, Germany, Great Britain, France, Italy and Canada).

GDP   Gross domestic product is the value of the sum of the goods and services produced by a country.

government securities   Treasury bills (short-term), notes (mid-term) and bonds (long-term) issued by the U.S. Government. Principal and interest are guaranteed by the taxing power of the U.S. Government. The most conservative form of investments because they are riskless that means they will pay lower interest rates than their private industry counterparts. Savings bonds are included in this class of investments.

greater fool theory   Concept that one who makes a skeptical investment will be able to sell that investment to a bigger fool.

gross margin   Total sales divided by the cost to produce those sales expressed as a percentage. A software company has a gross margin of 80 percent because its product is intellectual property, and it is inexpensive to reproduce. A noteworthy amount of money will be available for research and development, sales and marketing. A manufacturing firm that has a gross margin of 40 percent is resource impoverished. A large gross margin can provide money to aggressively pursue growth whereas a skimpy gross margin shrinks possibilities. One should monitor, quarterly and annually, the company's gross margin movement. If gross margins decline, a red flag may be hoisting up the pole. You should examine the causes and project the short and intermediate-term prospects.

house call   A notice from a broker to a customer that the margin account is deficient. When you buy on margin you are using the securities as collateral, and if the value of the securities declines to a specified level, the customer will have to deposit additional money or stock.

illiquid   A stock that exhibits low trading volume with noncompetitive pricing and volatility.

index fund   A mutual fund that owns a group of stocks modeled to copy the performance of a market or one of its sectors. It is passively managed with a low expense ratio. Compare the index fund with a similar investment for three, five and ten-year intervals.

IPO   An initial public offering occurs when a company, for the first time, issues shares to be sold to the public. The securities and not recommended for novice investors.

IRA   An individual retirement account created to fund retirement. In a traditional IRA one receives a tax deduction for eligible investments and pays taxes on the funds at distribution. A Roth IRA does not receive a tax deduction at inception; it is funded with post-tax dollars, and when is cashed in, it is tax free.

IRA Rollover   Assets receive from a retirement plan are transferred to an IRA.

January effect   The belief that stock prices will rise in January because prices were depressed in December as a result of selling for tax reasons, plus the addition of retirement funds flowing into the market. The January effect does not cause ticker prices to rise. Many variables impact equity prices, and it is hazardous to place bets based on history.

junk bond   A bond with investment credit rating of BB or lower. The credit report indicates there is above average risk that the company will be unable to make payments. Be alert in buying these bonds in recessionary or sluggish periods. They present greater default exposure. One should review the interest rate spread between junk bonds and investment quality bonds. Does the higher rate of the junk bond compensates for the additional risk?

leading economic indicators   An economic indicator that measures variations in the economy before changes exists. Money supply, building permits, unemployment insurance, stock prices and inventory shifts are examples of leading economic indicators.

limit order   A bid to buy a security at a specified limit or better. If one enters a limit order to buy 100 shares of XXX At $10.00, the order will be executed at $10.00 or less.

load fund   A mutual fund sold by a salesperson in which sales charges will be deducted from your investment. Do you receive good value for the sales charges you are paying? Can you duplicate the service and apply the sales charges to your investments?

Managed account   A person places money with a company to individually invest according to the needs and desires of the investor. The concept is personalized service with a firm that is smarter and luckier than other firms. The fees are swollen. Use the same approach that you would to grade a mutual fund. Select three, five, and ten-year terms for performance and compare with a similar investment.

margin account   A brokerage firm account where securities are bought on credit. Margin requirements are regulated by the Federal Reserve. If the margin qualification is 50 percent, one must post 50% of the transaction in cash. If the security decreases in value, you may be subject to a house call. You will pay interest on your margin balance. Margin interest rates vary from firm to firm. *It pays to shop them.*

market capitalization   The total value of all shares outstanding of a public corporation.

market order   A directive to buy or sell a security at the best price available.

money   It is a mind creation of a divine nature. Money has two purposes; you can count it or exchange it for goods and services. Money does not have an inherent value but a value based on our belief. If plentiful people believe a currency has value, the belief becomes operative. Money is supported by an idea of consensus, a product born of the mind not of the earth.

money-market   A mutual fund that pays dividends earned from high-quality short-term investments.

mortgage-backed securities   Fixed income wares that are backed by payments from real estate mortgages. Ginnie Mae bonds are the most secure since they are guaranteed by the U.S. Government for payment of principal and interest. Fannie Mae and Freddie Mac Bonds have a AAA credit rating, and are issued by government sponsored entities that have the implied backing of the U.S. Government. They have a line of credit with the Treasury Department. Financial institutions disperse mortgage-backed securities that are AAA rated. *If you shop interest rates, you will get a better deal and put more dollars in your pocket.*

muni   A municipal bond issued by a state, local government, or agency. It is nontaxable to residents of the state where purchased and of high credit quality.

Mutual fund   An investment company that sells and buys its shares on a regular basis. The money collected from the sale of its shares is invested in securities and cash. Capital gains and dividends are distributed to shareholders. *Inspect funds that have low expense ratios and a consistency of outperforming their adversaries over three, five, and ten-year slices of time.*

NAV   The net asset value of the mutual fund is the total value of the securities and cash at the end of the trading day.

NASDAQ   The computerized arrangement where over-the-counter stocks and several listed stocks are traded. The organization is comprised of broker/dealers who make the market in the stock and trade with the public.

no-load funds   Mutual funds without sales charges. They may have other lower expenses than load funds. Sales fees are OK if you believe you have received adequate value. You can educate yourself and pick mutual funds successfully or pay for the service. *You can do a better job of attending to your money than a salesperson, and the full force of your money will work for you.*

overconfidence   An investor behavior that creates the belief that one is brilliant in decision-making that results in excellent investment pay offs. Objective thought is ejected and the investor believes Zeus is his travel companion. With glazed eyes, he walks the road of suicide.

oversold   The belief that the market has experienced a span of selling that is not warranted with the implication that stocks are a bargain. Gibberish. A statement made with fondness by Augur Cockermouth. The price of the market is the price of the market, and can not be oversold unless you can predict the morrow.

passive investor   One who is not actively involved in managing his money. This can be accomplished by the purchase of mutual funds that are actively managed or index funds that are not actively managed. The index funds are the lowest cost vehicle. Compare different funds for three, five, and ten year stretches.

penny stock   A stock that sells for less than $5.00. Investigate why the bite is less than $5.00. Consider the volatility and riskiness of the venture. Design a plan of when to sell.

preferred stock   A stipulated cash flow vested interest that pays a dividend. It behaves closer to a bond than a common stock.

P/E   The price to earnings ratio of a stock. If a stock earns $2.00 per share and is trading at $20.00, the P/E is ten. The most popular yardstick evaluation of an equity. One must be comfortable with the truthfulness of the financial reports because the validity of the P/E rests on these reports. It is perilous to use the P/E as a prime instrument in the buying/selling verdict. The P/E informs you about to a moment in time and it is deficient about the horizon.

P/E/G   The ratio of the price of the stock to its earnings, and to its growth. If the P/E is ten and the expected earnings expansion is 15%/year, the stock is believed to be a good buy because earnings multiplication is forecast to outpace the P/E. The bugaboo is expected earnings. You may calculate what you like; the future is unwritten.

pro-forma earnings   An report that has been buffed and polished to present results that sketch a favorable drawing. Investment income or one time gains from unrelated business activities may be injected to pump up earnings. *Beware.*

prospectus   A detailed document offering securities for sale. It explains the business plan and presents financial information. This is the most objective report you will receive from management because of legal requirements for form and truthfulness. It is wise to highlight the section that deals with the possible briar patches the firm may face. Be observant of these minefields as the business enacts its story.

REIT   It is a business that gathers money from people to buy and manage income producing real estate or mortgage loans. REIT trade as common stock or mutual funds. The profits from operations are disseminated as dividends. These securities tend to be less volatile than other common stock. With attractive yields, consider them for the income section of your portfolio.

relative risk   A critical element of the investment puzzle. Each investments embodies degrees of risk, i.e. there can be a partial or total loss or a small gain. Seek to measure the risk components of similar investments. If you assume a greater risk in an investment, you are desirous to be compensated with greater reward. If you buy the stock of a company that manufactures facial tissues, you may assume annualized yields of 7 to 8%. If you partake in a company that creates business software, you will be looking for gains of 20% or greater. A business software firm operates in a steep risk environment where they are a program away from oblivion. People continue to sneeze.

sell-side analyst   A person employed by an investment firm to write reports to stimulate the buying of securities the firm wishes to sell. These analysts can produce quality work that can be a section of the maze.

Standard and Poor's 500   A bin of stocks of large companies, mostly U.S., representing growth and value equities across major industries.

Spider   A security traded on the American Stock Exchange that tracks the Standard and Poor's 500. It is an alternative to an index mutual fund having the advantages of trading as a common stock.

stop order   An order that is executed when a security reaches a specified price. When the directive is triggered, the transaction is done at the next best price.

time value   The concept that the worth of money is influenced by time. The investor has a finite number of years of existence on earth and his union membership card may expire in a moment. When one receives a accural on investment quickly, one can assume a modest result with reduced risk. When one waits for a longer period of time, one can envisage a greater profit with larger risk. Inflation erodes money. The money one owns today can be put to work while money receive later will be worth less.

uncertainty   With the exception of Treasury Securities, CD's and Ginnie Maes, you will be inviting the chance of loss into your house. Accept unpredictability as a fixture of the landscape.

upgrade   A sell-side analysts declares a stock to have improved prospects. *Beware.*

volatility   The movement of price in a security. Volatile stocks that are fueled with high octane pose greater risk. Speed creates and speed destroys; assure your saddle fits before you mount.

zero coupon   A stationary income product that deletes interest until maturation when the interest is paid with the principal. It is a popular tool to fund approaching expenses. You will pay taxes annually on interest earned and inflation will diminish your results.

0-595-27141-3

www.ingramcontent.com/pod-product-compliance
Lightning Source LLC
Chambersburg PA
CBHW030759180526
45163CB00003B/1094